**Legal Issues in
Addict Diversion**

Legal Issues in Addict Diversion

Harvey Perlman
University of Virginia

Peter Jaszi
The American University

Lexington Books
D.C. Heath and Company
Lexington, Massachusetts
Toronto   London

Library of Congress Cataloging in Publication Data

Perlman, Harvey S   1942-
    Legal issues in addict diversion.

    Includes bibliographical references.
    1. Narcotic addicts—Legal status, laws, etc.—United States. I.
Jaszi, Peter, joint author. II. Title.
KF3829.N2P4 1976   334'.73'04463   75-43474
ISBN 0-669-00568-1

Published simultaneously in Canada

Printed in the United States of America

International Standard Book Number: 0-669-00568-1

Library of Congress Catalog Card Number: 75-43474

KF
3829
.N2
P4
1976

Contents

Foreword

In late 1974, the Drug Abuse Council and the Commission on Correctional Facilities and Services joined in publication of a "layman's guide" on legal issues in addict diversion. That short monograph, designed for nonlawyer professionals, planners, treatment staff, program administrators, and researchers working in the addict diversion field, was enthusiastically received.

This book offers a technical legal analysis, with extensive citations, on the same subject. Designed primarily for lawyers seeking to deal with legal aspects of addict diversion programs, it is hoped that it serves as useful a function as the layman's guide.

What the sponsors had occasion to say with respect to the earlier publication holds equally as well for this technical monograph. The problem of extensive nonmedical use of psychoactive drugs continues and the law enforcement, social, and medical implications of such drug-using behavior remain complex and interrelated. Diversion programs for drug users, which provide for systematic referral of individuals from the criminal justice system to treatment, maintain their popularity as an alternative response to drug abuse problems and present their special dilemmas in the ongoing quest for accommodation of new treatment knowledge and understanding with established procedures of law and constitutional rights.

The legal issues discussed here in depth are, it may be said, the "skirmish points" for structuring the well-defined relationship needed to assure that the sometimes conflicting objectives of effective treatment services and criminal justice principles are reconciled in a manner permitting sound programs to operate and individual rights to be protected and preserved.

This book, like its earlier counterpart, is a product of the National Pretrial Intervention Service Center whose consultant co-authors have provided this challenging and comprehensive analysis. While the general topic coverage is similar to the layman's guide, some of the didactic text of the guide explaining constitutional protections and judicial concepts has been omitted and a more sophisticated level of analysis introduced.

This analysis makes it quite clear that the major legal problems posed by the implementation of diversion programs exist in milieus where clear solutions are often elusive and the law has yet to be concretely defined and applied. However, issues and alternatives are laid out, positive answers and conclusions are articulated where this seems reasonably possible, and the concepts by which eventual resolution of difficult issues may be approached are suggested.

The council and the commission are indeed pleased to have supported this project in furtherance of their hope that the concept of "addict diversion" as a humane, effective, and just alternative to criminal conviction and incarceration can be further refined and accepted as a permanent component of the criminal justice process.

ROBERT B. McKAY, *Chairman*
Commission on Correctional Facilities & Services

THOMAS E. BRYANT, *President*
Drug Abuse Council, Inc.

Washington, D.C.

Preface

The manuscript for this work resulted from the encouragement and sponsorship of the Drug Abuse Council, Inc. and the National Pretrial Intervention Service Center of the American Bar Association Commission on Correctional Facilities and Services. An initial publication entitled *Legal Issues in Addict Diversion: A Layman's Guide* was published jointly by the sponsors and was designed to explain to nonlawyers in diversion programs some of the legal implications of their activities. We were then encouraged by both agencies to develop a more technical analysis of the legal doctrines that might impinge on the growing use of addict diversion techniques.

While the manuscript was originally published by the sponsoring agencies in softbound form in early 1975, we have found it necessary to update the material in this edition in several areas. Of major significance: we have revised chapter 2 in light of the reversal by the United States Court of Appeals of the District of Columbia of the lower court ruling in *Committee for G.I. Rights* v. *Callaway*, which had invalidated the U.S. Army's drug detection program. We have also revised in some detail parts of chapter 6 to take into account new rules adopted by the secretary of Health, Education, and Welfare to protect the confidentiality of patient records in drug abuse programs.

Since diversion programs have for the most part operated informally for many years, the courts have not had the opportunity to examine directly the legal issues arising out of these programs. We have thus tried to consider a wide range of legal concepts in arguably analogous cases in order to speculate on their applicability to the special context of addict diversion. We have, in several instances, considered at length cases or constitutional doctrines that we ultimately conclude are not applicable. To the accusation that we may have raised straw men we plead guilty. However, since the work is one that explores generally untraveled paths, we determined to err on the side of inclusion.

It will become clear to those who venture further in this work that we have not set about the task of defending the existing framework for diversion programs. Indeed, in many areas we express our deep concern that the current means employed to handle drug abusers more sensibly may be shown to encompass infringements of individual rights. We are not oblivious to the fact that in some areas we urge caution based on an extension of the United States Supreme Court cases at a time when the present Court seems bent on more restrictive interpretations. Our hope is that we have adequately raised the lurking issues of individual rights so that they will be protected, if not by the courts, by the legislatures or by the policies and practices of diversion personnel.

We are indebted to our two sponsoring agencies and particularly to Dan Skoler and Arnold Hopkins of the American Bar Association Commission, who with admirable tact and patience at time assisted and at times cajoled us toward completion. We are also grateful for the assistance of student researchers Edward Levin and Stephan Gray. The views, opinions, and mistakes contained in this work are exclusively our own.

**Legal Issues in
Addict Diversion**

1 Introduction

The impetus toward establishment of "addict-diversion" programs in American criminal procedure represents a convergence of three significant tendencies in thinking about problems of criminal justice and drug abuse: increased concern over the incidence of habitual narcotics use and drug-related crime, enhanced dissatisfaction with the quality of justice generally available in trial courts, and growing public confidence in the effectiveness of new modes of noninstitutional treatment for drug dependency.[1] During the 1960s, planning for "alternative treatment" of drug-dependent persons charged with criminal offenses emphasized schemes for long- or medium-term institutional "civil commitment" exemplified by the programs conducted by the California Rehabilitation Center at Corona and the dispersed facilities of the New York State Narcotics Addiction Control Commission. By the end of the decade, however, the high costs of the program, together with the ambiguous records of accomplishment they had compiled, had brought their real value into serious question. In some degree, the movement toward addict diversion may be explained as a movement away from the commitment model.

Unlike the civil-commitment programs, addict diversion programs are designed to identify drug-dependent defendants in the earliest phases of the criminal process and to channel certain of the defendants out of the criminal justice system before their cases have proceeded any distance toward disposition. Also, unlike the civil-commitment programs, addict-diversion programs do not recruit patient–clients by outright coercion. The defendant considered eligible for addict diversion is offered an opportunity to "volunteer;" with his or her acceptance of that opportunity, the pending prosecution is suspended or deferred for a period of months. If the divertee "succeeds" in treatment during the diversion period, he or she in turn receives—by prearrangement—either an outright dismissal of the pending charges, or some other significant concession from the prosecuting authorities. Although the nature and quality of the "voluntarism" of addict diversion is open to question, it can at least be said that no defendant is compelled to participate over his or her objection. Finally, unlike the civil-commitment programs, addict-diversion programs aim to accomplish their therapeutic goals through encouraging relatively short periods of supervised participation in noninstitutional therapies, such as outpatient methadone maintenance or therapeutic community residence.

1

The major catalyst for the implementation of diversion programs for drug addicts has been the Special Action Office for Drug Abuse Prevention, which began planning a national "Treatment Alternatives to Street Crime" (TASC) program in late 1971. Through funding by the Law Enforcement Assistance Administration and the National Institute of Mental Health, projects became operational in Wilmington, Delaware and Philadelphia, Pennsylvania in late 1972. As of December 1, 1974, 26 TASC programs had been funded with two additional applications under review. On this date there were 3,138 clients in treatment with 8,271 having been served by a TASC program. Agency projections indicate that by June of 1975, over 13,000 persons will have been processed, with the possibility of funding of additional projects across the country. These figures account for only persons involved in programs funded under the TASC programs.[2]

Considered as an innovation in criminal case processing, addict diversion is a mixed medical–legal service. The complex medical issues it poses are beyond the scope of this work, although further investigations of the comparative performance of addict–divertees in various forms of treatment are urgently required. The emerging legal issues, upon which this book focuses, are generally the same as those presented by the wide range of new programs designed to provide general rehabilitative services to nonaddicted defendants on deferred prosecution status — programs generally described as practical experiments in "pretrial probation." But an examination of the practice of addict diversion reveals these issues in particularly sharp terms.

In addict diversion, as contrasted to other models of pretrial intervention, the defendant–divertee is competing for particularly high stakes: while most pretrial-intervention programs limit their client populations to accused misdemeants, addict-diversion programs regularly accept defendants facing far more serious potential criminal penalties; where most pretrial-intervention programs entail a suspension of prosecution for only 30 to 90 days, the typical addict–divertee is required to accept a suspension of 6 to 12 months; although all diversion programs generate records concerning their clients, the records generated in the course of drug-abuse therapy are of a particular sensitive nature. Even more clearly than participants in other forms of pretrial-intervention programming, the potential addict–divertee is faced with a valuable opportunity to avoid the direct and collateral consequences of conviction while securing positive services; equally clear, however, are the enhanced disadvantages to a potential addict–divertee from recruitment into an inequitably or ineptly managed program, or arbitrary exclusion from an otherwise sound program. In the design and administration of addict-diversion programs, considerations of equality in access, procedural fairness, availability of legal counsel, and preservation of confidentiality deserve special consideration.

The choices faced by program planners weighing each of these considerations are susceptible to both legal and policy analysis. In the interest of the programs, the clients, and society at large, designers of addict-diversion programs may be well advised to provide a number of substantive and procedural safeguards even where those safeguards are not unambiguously mandated by a principle of constitutional or statute law. Many of the issues raised by addict-diversion programs have not as yet been the subject of direct litigation. However, it seems reasonably clear that current practices will come under increased scrutiny by the courts. This book explores some of the widely divergent issues that may arise from such scrutiny.

In this book, addict diversion is treated primarily as a generic phenomenon. In practice, of course, details of individual diversion programs vary significantly between—and even within—jurisdictions. But in order to analyze the legal implications of the addict-diversion phenomenon, and to mark the legal pitfalls around which planners must negotiate, it has proved convenient to frame the discussion in terms of a composite portrait of an addict-diversion program. Not every operating addict-diversion program, for example, is actively engaged in testing recent arrestees for the ephemeral traces of recent narcotics use; some recruit solely from among self-identified addict–defendants. But a significant number of programs—or proposals for programs—do include an "addict-identification" component operating in local detention facilities. Thus, in devising the composite portrait of an addict-diversion program to which this work refers, an addict-identification phase or component has been included.

In brief, the principal phases of the composite addict-diversion program are as follows:

Addict identification. By means of chemical testing, medical examinations, and interviews, program personnel attempt to determine which newly arrested persons are habitual drug users and thus possible candidates for addict diversion.

Treatment-conditioned Pretrial Release. As a measure intermediate between mere identification of addict defendants and acceptance of certain of them into a diversion program on a deferred prosecution basis, addict–defendants are encouraged to participate in treatment while awaiting disposition of their cases. Typically, the mechanism will be a judicial order mandating participation in treatment or supervised abstinence as a condition of pretrial release on personal recognizance, cash bail, or bond. Recruitment for diversion itself may be limited to those addict-defendants who have both qualified for pretrial release on this basis and demonstrated good faith by complying with the treatment conditions imposed.

Diversion Intake. Potential candidates for addict diversion are screened for eligibility. Typically, such screening involves two subphases. In the first, candidates are eliminated because they fail to satisfy one or more pre-determined eligibility criteria. In the second, others are eliminated because they fail to satisfy a decision maker that they are good prospects for rehabilitation in lieu of prosecution. Those addict–defendants who survive both phases of the screening will be offered an opportunity to participate in diversion; at this point, the terms on which participation is available, the potential risks of participation, and the benefits that will or may be conferred on divertees upon successful completion of the program are explained. Any paperwork associated with acceptance—including the execution of form waivers—is completed. Diversion is formally accomplished by a motion for continuance or a limited suspension of further proceedings.

Treatment. The divertee is assigned to a designated addiction therapy program, which may be one accepting referrals from a variety of sources in addition to the criminal courts. His or her progress in treatment is monitored by means of periodic reports from the treatment-delivery agency to the diverting authority. Among the most important devices employed in assessing the performance of divertees in treatment is urinalysis—performed either on a regular or spot-check basis—to detect traces of illicit drug use.

Termination of diversion. In the event that a divertee completes the diversion period in a manner that satisfies the program's working definition of "success in treatment," he or she receives the benefit profferred by the diverting authority at intake—typically, a dismissal of pending charges accomplished either by unilateral prosecutorial action of by a motion to the court in which the case is pending. In the event of a divertee's "failure"— which may be a lack of progress in treatment, a refusal to cooperate in administrative routines associated with treatment, or a violation of the terms of the diversion such as rearrest—he or she is returned to the criminal justice system, and prosecution on the pending charges is resumed.

Although many of the legal considerations involved in addict-diversion programs are relatively complex in nature and troublesome in their implications, none appears to afford the basis for a legal challenge to the concept of addict diversion itself.[3] Nor do all the questions raised below concerning the legal legitimacy of practices associated with addict diversion—even when taken together—afford the basis for such a sweeping challenge. Instead, they offer the starting point for dialogue and discussion concerning the proper design of addict-diversion programs.

Notes

1. For an account of the origins of "addict diversion" and the major program models, see Note, *Addict Diversion: An Alternative Approach for the Criminal Justice System*, 60 GEO. L.J. 667 (1972). See also Note, *Diversion of Drug Offenders in California*, 26 STAN. L. REV. 923 (1974).

2. For a background discussion of TASC, see LEAA White Paper, The National Treatment Alternatives to Street Crime Program, July 15, 1974. Client counts are distributed in a monthly bulletin prepared by the Narcotics and Drug Abuse Program Coordinator, Office of Regional Operations, LEAA. The bulletin is entitled *TASC TALK*.

3. This book does not purport to consider the merits of diversion programs in the treatment of addicts or as a permanent feature of the criminal justice system.

2

Legal Issues in Addict Identification: Drug-use Interviews and Urinalysis

The most troubling constitutional objections to present addict-diversion programs arise out of the procedures employed by program representatives to identify addicts among those persons arrested in a given jurisdiction. Most addict-diversion programs have the objective of actively recruiting candidates for addiction treatment from the pool of arrestees who might not come forward of their own initiative. To serve this objective, these programs have adopted procedures that make screening for drug dependency—by physical examinations, drug-use interviews and urinalysis—uniformly applicable to all arrested persons. Because indicative chemical traces of recent drug use are evanescent, and because many drug-dependent arrestees will not request diversion while their dependence remains undiscovered, a program that aims to include all arrestees in the "catchment" population for diversion to treatment must not delay addict identification until after individual defendants have expressed interest in the diversion option. In those programs relying on self-identified drug users, it is still necessary to verify their admissions of drug dependency by independent testing. Thus, urinalysis and drug-use interviews are standard procedures in many existing diversion programs.[1]

Before noting the features of early addict identification techniques that are open to challenge on constitutional grounds, it is useful to review the legal, physical, and psychological milieu in which these techniques exist and the purposes for which examination results are employed. Only in this context can the potential for infringement of the rights of defendants by uniform addict-identification procedures be assessed.

When first approached by a representative of an addict-diversion program, or by a law enforcement officer delegated to cooperate in addict-identification screening, a defendant is in prearraignment custody—in a police lockup, a local jail, or a central courthouse holding pen. He probably has been arrested during the last 24 hours; in the time since his arrest he has undergone a full body search and has participated in a battery of compulsory "self-identification" procedures, including finger-printing, photography, and the solicitation of miscellaneous personal data. In addition, he may have submitted to a variety of more intrusive identification procedures, including lineups, "showups," and physical examinations conducted for medical or investigatory purposes. The defendant in prear-

7

raignment detention has been notified of his right to counsel; usually, however, the indigent defendant is not yet actually represented by an appointed attorney at this stage of the criminal process. Depending on local practice, the defendant may or may not have been informed of the specific content of the formal charge that will be lodged against him at arraignment; in every jurisdiction, however, he is awaiting the pretrial release hearing, which may be in practice the most critical early stage in the criminal process.

The individual who initiates the addict-identification process typically will be a "counsellor" or "screener" attached to a diversion project, a court probation officer, or a staff member of a drug-treatment program; although he may identify himself to the defendant as unaffiliated with police or prosecution, their encounter takes place in a custodial setting, under the supervision of law enforcement personnel.[2] On occasion, the individual initiating the screening may be a police officer with custodial responsibility at the lockup where the defendant is being held.

In general, the defendant is requested to give a urine sample and is informed that an analysis of this sample will show his recent use of illicit drugs, if any. In addition, he is requested to supply a verbal account of his drug use in response to a series of questions concerning the types of drugs used, the frequency and pattern with which they are used, the amount and expense of drugs consumed, and the duration of the defendant's drug-use history. In some addict-diversion programs, the interview may precede the request for a urine sample; in others, interviewing may be delayed until urinalysis results have been received. In almost every program, however, both urine sampling and interviewing are essential elements of the screening technique.[3] Urinalysis alone can establish only that an individual has consumed drugs (including narcotics, barbituates, amphetamines, and alcohol) during the 24 to 48 hours preceding sampling; only an interview can establish whether the drug was used pursuant to a prescription, on an extraordinary one-time basis, or as part of a pattern of habitual or compulsive drug abuse. On occasion, visual observations of a defendant may supplement urinalysis results or interview data (as when obvious withdrawal symptoms or needle "tracks" indicate past heroin use), but a defendant's first-hand account of his drug history generally is regarded as necessary to a determination of his eligibility for diversion to treatment.

When first contact between the screener and the defendant is made, the screener ordinarily will:

1. Outline the general purposes for which the test and interview results are being sought
2. Provide assurances that results will not be employed for prosecutorial purposes[4]

3. Advise that a defendant's failure to cooperate in tests and interviews will be brought to the attention of the judicial officer presiding at arraignment, and may be given adverse weight in the pretrial release decision.

The defendant ordinarily will not be advised of a right to the advice of counsel during addict identification tests or interviews.

Once secured, urinalysis test results and a summary of interview data are presented in open court at the defendant's first court hearing. Copies ordinarily are provided to all parties, including, of course, the prosecutor. In addition, a copy is filed in the case's file jacket to become a permanent part of the court record in the proceedings.

Two legal questions of considerable importance appear from a review of the typical addict-identification routine: (1) May participation in urinalysis and drug-use interviews be compelled; and (2) under what conditions can a defendant in custodial detention effectively waive whatever constitutional rights might be infringed by compulsory participation in addict-identification procedures? Although neither of these issues has been litigated to date, court challenges to addict-identification procedures must be anticipated as the addict-diversion concept gains increasing currency. The likely lines along which these issues would be resolved in the courts, as they appear from constitutional principles and analogous case-law authority, are crucial, both to the design of new addict-diversion programs and the revision of operating protocols for existing programs.

Compulsory Drug-use Interviews

The Fifth Amendment prohibits the government from compelling a person to incriminate himself by providing testimony that would serve as a "link in the chain of evidence" used to charge him with criminal conduct. Compelled drug-use interviews would seem to run contrary to this basic constitutional principle. The information sought in these interviews can be incriminating evidence of criminal conduct. While addiction to narcotics by itself cannot be the subject of criminal penalties,[5] an admission of addiction carries with it, expressly or by implication, the further admission that a defendant has engaged in conduct that can be made criminal, that is, possession of prohibited substances. A defendant, regardless of the charge for which he was originally arrested, may reasonably entertain the apprehension that his admission of prior drug use itself may be the basis for further investigation leading to a drug-law prosecution. Even if no direct evidentiary use is made of a defendant's admission of addiction, that admission may nevertheless mark him as a target for intensified future surveillance. The admission of drug use thus gives the prosecution an investigative "lead".

While the Fifth Amendment appears on its face to create a privilege limited to compelling testimonial evidence during the trial of a criminal case, the courts long ago recognized the potentially incriminating nature of statements made to a variety of other government initiated inquiries.[6] On the other hand, all disclosures compelled by the government are not protected by the Fifth Amendment.[7] In short, it now appears that the need for the privilege must be balanced against the needs of the government for the information.

The Regulation Cases

There are two lines of cases that shed some light on the factors affecting the application of the Fifth Amendment to drug-use interviews. In a series of cases beginning with *Albertson* v. *SACB*,[8] and *Marchetti* v. *United States*,[9] the Supreme Court held that certain statutory schemes requiring registration violated the privilege. In *Albertson* the Court struck down an order directing individual members of the Communist party to register with the government. In *Marchetti* the Court invalidated the registration provisions of the federal wagering tax statutes. In subsequent cases, registration provisions involving gambling and unlicensed firearms were declared in violation of the privilege.[10] In all of these cases disclosure of the information was found to "significantly enhance the likelihood of their prosecution for future acts."[11] The thrust of these opinions is that compliance with government compelled questions during registration would force the person to run the real risk of incrimination, something the Fifth Amendment prohibits.

However, in the recent case of *California* v. *Byers*,[12] the Supreme Court significantly limited the scope of *Marchetti* in approving a state statute requiring self-reporting by drivers involved in property damage accidents. The plurality opinion, concurred in by only four justices, distinguished the *Marchetti* line of cases. The Court noted that the statute in *Byers* was essentially regulatory and not criminal, that the statute was directed at the public-at-large rather than a "highly selective group inherently suspect of criminal activities," that driving an automobile is a "lawful activity," that the purpose of the statute was noncriminal, and that the reporting provisions were necessary to fulfill the noncriminal purpose. The Court did recognize, however, that the driver's identification might "lead to inquiry that in turn leads to arrest and charge."

Justice Harlan concurred in the result but not in the plurality opinion. He formulated his own balancing formula, which included three factors: "... the assertedly noncriminal governmental purpose in securing the information, the necessity for self-reporting, and the nature of the disclosures required." [13] These factors were to be balanced in light of the purposes of the Fifth Amendment, which were fundamentally designed to preserve the accusatorial system of criminal jurisprudence. In distinguishing the hit-and-run reporting statute from those declared invalid in *Marchetti*, Justice Harlan emphasized that the government was using the taxing system as a device to pursue the criminal sanction, and the answers required in the self-reporting systems were direct admissions of criminal involvement. In *Byers*, however, he argued that the major purpose was in fact regulatory, that the state had required a minimal disclosure (name and address) and that after that disclosure, the state still had the prosecutorial obligation to prove that the actions of the driver were in fact criminal.

The split of opinion on the Court makes *Byers* a difficult case to interpret.[14] However, it is doubtful that under either the plurality opinion or that of Justice Harlan, compulsory drug interviews would survive a Fifth Amendment challenge. Regarding the plurality formulation, the information disclosed involving drug use is not a "lawful activity" like driving an automobile; the interviews are given to a "highly suspect group," that is, those already arrested under criminal charges; and although the purpose of the disclosure is noncriminal, diversion programs for the most part are directly tied to criminal justice officials. The information obtained from such interviews would create a real likelihood of incrimination. Justice Harlan's formula would appear to lead to a similar result. While the governmental purpose for drug-use interviews is noncriminal in a broad sense, it is an integral part of the prosecution of the offense for which the person was arrested.

In *Byers*, the argument was offered that the disclosure could be compelled if the state would agree not to use the disclosed information in subsequent criminal prosecutions. This was rejected by the plurality and Justice Harlan, the latter noting that granting immunity would as a practical matter disrupt the regulation of automobile driving. In addict diversion, however, the granting of use immunity is not of the same character. The information obtained in the interviews may or may not relate to the offense for which the person is arrested. In an analogous context, the Congress in 1972 legislation appeared to recognize that record confidentiality for addicts in treatment was not necessarily antagonistic to prosecutorial interests.[15]

Finally, the nature of the disclosure required in a drug-use interview is closer to the type compelled in *Marchetti* than to the minimal information required in *Byers*. In *Byers*, the driver had to indicate his name and address, which, in turn, indicated he was involved in the accident. However, in the drug-use interviews, the interviewee is asked about his involvement with drugs. The disclosure has a direct connection with illegal activity.

The Pretrial Psychiatric Examination Cases

The tension between the personal constitutional privilege against self-incrimination and the state's interest in obtaining useful and otherwise unavailable data concerning defendants, which is implicit in the prearraignment addict-identification interview, has been litigated in the arguably analogous context of the court-ordered pretrial mental examination. Like the addict-identification interview, the mental examination is not *intended* to compel or coerce disclosure of directly incriminating admissions; like the addict-identification interview, a typical court-ordered mental examination is conducted in a custodial setting, but by professional specialists who, while they may be full- or part-time state employees, are not members of the prosecution "team" as such; like the addict-identification interview, the mental examination cannot succeed without the cooperation of the subject, which cooperation can be encouraged by the use of a battery of express or implied threats and inducements.[16]

The pretrial psychiatric examination occurs in two distinguishable contexts. The court may order such an examination to determine if the accused is presently competent, that is, whether he is mentally capable of assisting his counsel with his defense. If he is incompetent in this regard, the trial cannot continue. Competency to stand trial goes directly to the issue of a fair trial, and it is generally the responsibility of the prosecution and the court to raise the issue if either suspects incompetency.

If an accused pleads insanity as a defense to the criminal act, the court may order psychiatric examinations by court appointed expert witnesses or those selected by the prosecution. In this context, the accused has raised the issue of his insanity at the time of the offense, and a finding of insanity precludes conviction.

For purposes of considering these cases' applicability to drug-use interviews, it is important to recognize that in the competency to stand trial context, the examination may be ordered without the request or other action of the defendant. This is closer to the situation where all arrested individuals are subjected to interviews. The insanity defense cases involve the assertion of a specific defense by the accused, and many courts have considered this a waiver of any Fifth Amendment rights involved in psychiatric examinations. These latter cases may be more relevant to considerations of waiver where drug-use interviews are a prerequisite to admission to a diversion program since a request to participate in diversion might be considered a waiver of Fifth Amendment objections.

In the federal courts the ordering of a pretrial psychiatric examination for purposes of determining competency to stand trial is governed by 18 U.S.C. § 4244, which authorizes the court on its own motion to order such an examination. That statute reads in part:

No statement made by the accused in the course of any examination into his sanity or mental competency provided for by this section, whether the examination shall be with or without consent of the accused, shall be admitted in evidence against the accused on the issue of guilt in any criminal proceeding.

The appellate courts, which have ruled directly on the permissibility of such court-ordered examinations, in the face of a Fifth Amendment challenge have upheld the compelled examination relying on the immunity granted by the above quoted passage.[17] Thus, for these cases to stand in support of compelled drug-use interviews, a comparable grant of immunity would be required.

For those addict-diversion programs authorized or assisted under the provisions of the Federal Drug Abuse Office and Treatment Act of 1972, it has been argued that a comparable if not more extensive immunity provision exists.[18] However, leaving the immunity question aside, the case for drug-use interviews is hardly as compelling as pretrial psychiatric examinations when the competency of the accused to present a defense is at issue. Absent the examination or some other determination of competency, the trial itself cannot proceed with the assurance that it will be fair. And the government, as well as the accused, has an interest in a fair trial.

On the other hand, prohibitions against drug-use interviews of every arrestee may make more difficult the identification of addicts, which in turn may mean that some may not be identified for drug treatment.[19] No one argues that treatment received during diversion is a panacea for drug addiction or that it is provably successful in a large percentage of cases. The government's interest in assigning a person to a diversion program is hardly as great as bringing a person to trial for a committed offense. This is particularly true when it is recognized that the government cannot compel participation in the diversion program itself since persons eligible for diversion remain unconvicted of any crime and courts have generally ruled that such pretrial detainees have a right to avoid involuntary rehabilitation.[20]

There are more numerous cases involving the application of the Fifth Amendment privilege to ordered mental examinations when the defendant asserts that he was insane at the time he committed the offense. In this context, questions during the examination will be more sensitive since they will inevitably pursue activities at the time of the offense and are more likely to be incriminatory. In jurisdictions that have allowed such examinations, the possibility of incrimination has been minimized by a variety of procedures including special jury instructions,[21] bifurcated trial proceedings,[22] and limitations on the testimony of state-appointed examiners to nonincriminating matters.[23] However, the difficulty of balancing the Fifth Amendment privilege against the need of the prosecution for information to contest an insanity plea has been recognized. Some courts have authorized such compelled examinations on a variety of grounds.[24] Critical to the analysis of most courts is the fact that the accused, by pleading insanity, has created the necessity for the examination.[25]

There are, however, a few cases that even in the face of the prosecution's admitted predicament of being forced to contest evidence of insanity without the benefit of its own examination, have refused to authorize compelled examinations in light of the Fifth Amendment. In *Shepard* v. *Bowe*,[26] the Supreme Court of Oregon so held. The language of the court has particular significance for this analysis of the constitutionality of addict-identification interviews, since it emphasizes that in any compelled interview with representatives of the state, a defendant is in jeopardy of direct and indirect self-incrimination and that nothing short of a complete recognition of the defendant's privilege to refuse without penalty will provide adequate security against both risks:

Even if we prohibited the psychiatrist from testifying to incriminating statements made to him by the defendant in a pretrial mental examination, requiring the defendant to answer could nevertheless jeopardize the privilege against self-incrimination. The statements made by the defendant to the psychiatrist could provide a lead to other evidence which would incriminate the defendant on the issue of guilt. If the trial court ordered that statements made by the defendant to the psychiatrist could not be revealed to the state or to any other person except upon court order, we are of the opinion that under certain circumstances there is more than a remote chance that such statements would become known to others in addition to the trial court.[27]

The court's recognition that information once disclosed cannot be fully protected dictates cautious evaluation of pronouncements in diversion programs that confidentiality will be preserved.

Although there is a general state interest in identifying drug-dependent defendants, it cannot be analogized in urgency to the state interest in obtaining independent expert evidence concerning the mental state of specific defendants who assert particular claims relating to their psychological condition—an interest so strong that it may justify the substitution of limitations on use by recipients of privileged admissions for the defendants' unqualified privilege to refuse disclosure. The justification that "[t]he maintenance of a 'fair state-individual balance' clearly require[s] that the government be permitted to have the defendant examined [because] once the defendant [has] offered some evidence that he is not sane, the burden of proving legal sanity is on the government,"[28] is implicit in the psychiatric examination cases that have given the privilege less than full scope. It is inapposite to the problem of addict-identification interviews.

Immunity and the Fifth Amendment

The Fifth Amendment proscribes government conduct that forces an individual to testify in circumstances where there is a "substantial probability of incrimination" in criminal conduct.[29] If the government under appropriate guidelines is willing to forego use of the information in a criminal prosecution, it can punish the refusal to provide that information. The United States Supreme Court has upheld the concept of "use" immunity—the grant of immunity for compelled disclosures from their use or derivative use in any future criminal proceeding.[30] As the Court noted, where the prosecution seeks to prosecute a person who has testified under a grant of immunity it must bear the burden of showing "that the evidence it proposes to use is derived from a legitimate source wholly independent of the compelled testimony."[31] Under this rule the immunity granted is coextensive with the Fifth Amendment privilege—an essential prerequisite to the government compelling a person to testify.[32]

In *Kastigar* v. *United States,*[33] the Court upheld an immunity statute, which provided: "no testimony or other information compelled under the order (or any information directly or indirectly derived from such testimony or other information) may be used against the witness in any criminal case."[34] In *Zicarelli* v. *New Jersey State Commission of Investigation,* decided the same day as *Kastigar,* the Court upheld a grant of immunity with the following scope: "he shall be immune from having such responsive answer given by him or such responsive evidence by him or evidence derived therefrom used to expose him to criminal prosecution or penalty or to a forfeiture of his estate."[35] The Court noted that both statutes provided immunity from direct use of compelled testimony and from the use of other information derived from leads gained from the compelled testimony. Both use and derivative use must be prohibited before the Fifth Amendment privilege can be circumvented.

As indicated above, compulsory drug-use interviews are a direct violation of the Fifth Amendment and can be conducted only with an appropriate grant of immunity. In this way the compelled disclosures would not be "incriminatory." It remains to consider whether existing immunity authorization would effectively eliminate the incriminatory aspects of such interviews in the addict-diversion context.

Immunity Statutes. Section 408 of the Federal Drug Abuse Office and Treatment Act of 1972[36] contains what appears to be an immunity provision applicable to some addict-diversion programs. The section applies to drug-abuse prevention functions conducted, regulated, or directly or indirectly assisted by any department or agency of the United States.[37] The section grants a limited confidentiality to patient records arising out of a drug-abuse function. The legal analysis of TASC, prepared by grantees and distributed by the Special Action Office suggests that where Fifth Amendment difficulties arise, section 408 "establishes the rough equivalent of immunity" and "could, arguably, be the statutory basis to secure a grant of immunity and, upon refusal, to compel cooperation."[38]

The act applies only to records of the "identity, diagnosis, prognosis, or treatment of any patient." Current regulations expand the definition to any information obtained "incident to" diagnosis or treatment. The regulations also specifically include within the definition of "patient" a person "who after arrest on a criminal charge, is interviewed and/or tested in connection with drug . . . abuse preliminary to a determination as to eligibility to participate in a treatment or rehabilitation program."[39]

It is doubtful that the section grants immunity in a scope sufficient to meet the standards established by *Kastigar.* Subsection (c) provides:

Except as authorized by a court order granted under subsection (b) (2) (C) (for good cause shown) of this section, no record referred to in subsection (a) may be used to initiate or substantiate any criminal charges against a patient or to conduct any investigation of a patient.

The excepting clause authorizing a court order would take away from the immunity grant sufficient scope to prohibit it from being sufficient for Fifth Amendment purposes. While it might be contended that "good cause shown" could not be interpreted to include a violation of the Fifth Amendment, the structure of the subsection contemplates breach of immunity in some criminal prosecutions. To give any meaning to the exception for a court order necessarily requires an interpretation authorizing use in a criminal proceeding.

The regulations pursuant to the section purport to limit court ordered disclosure to "objective data" and to preclude any disclosure of "communications by a patient to program personnel." The validity of this regulation is considered in chapter 6. However even if valid, objective data derived from communications could be incriminatory.

Furthermore, it is questionable whether absent the exception the grant of immunity is coextensive with the Fifth Amendment privilege. While use seems to be prohibited, derivative use—using the information gained as a lead for further investigation—is arguably allowed. It is conceivable that a court could interpret the language "used . . . to conduct any investigation of a patient" as containing a full derivative use prohibition but the language of the section is certainly not as direct as that upheld by the Court in *Kastigar* and *Zicarelli.* The ambiguity of the scope of the immunity and the exception for the court order would appear to render the statute ineffective in overcoming the strictures of the Fifth Amendment.

There is no question that an immunity statute could be drafted to avoid the pitfalls inherent in drug-use interviews.[40] However, in the context of day-to-day drug-use law enforcement, the burden placed on the prosecution to establish an independent source for evidence used against the defendant once immunity is granted may prove impossible to meet. This, of course, might undercut prosecution support for addict-diversion programs.

Prosecution Promises of Immunity. In the absence of legislation authorizing immunity, some diversion programs may attempt to avoid application of the Fifth Amendment by program policy statements or guidelines that in effect promise immunity or confidentiality in exchange for participation in drug-use interviews. The purpose of this section is to consider what effect such promises would have regarding the Fifth Amendment privilege.

Only Texas has held directly that the prosecutor has inherent authority to grant immunity sufficient to eliminate a Fifth Amendment claim of privilege.[41] In most other states, the courts have refused to recognize such power arguing that the power to pardon is generally vested in the governor or chief executive.[42] Thus, in the absence of legislative authorization, promises of immunity by prosecutors are unauthorized.

However, the effect of such a promise arises in two separate contexts. Clearly an unauthorized promise of immunity is not a sufficient basis to impose sanctions for refusal to testify. Thus a witness can remain silent in the face of an unauthorized prosecution promise of immunity without fearing the imposition of sanctions.[43] Absent legislation, diversion-program guidelines that promise immunity are ineffective and pretrial detainees may continue to refuse to participate in drug-use interviews.

A more difficult question arises where persons in reliance on promises, although unauthorized, participate in drug-use interviews. It would seem that even though the prosecutor has no power to grant immunity, information obtained in reliance on a promise of immunity could not subsequently be used to incriminate the individual. The Illinois Supreme Court reversed a conviction based on a statement given under an invalid promise of immunity.[44] And, the United States Supreme Court, in the context of plea bargaining, has emphasized that prosecutorial promises should be binding as a matter of constitutional law.[45]

Compulsory Urinalysis

The second major component of early addict-identification testing procedures—urinalysis—creates closer and more difficult constitutional questions. Three separate possibilities exist for conducting a urinalysis testing program: (1) such tests can be given only to those who "volunteer";[46] (2) tests can be given only to those who there is reasonable evidence to suggest are narcotic users;[47] (3) tests can be given on a compulsory basis to all arrested individuals.[48] The latter two alternatives and particularly a program of compulsory testing of all arrestees create the most complex legal issues. Such programs must be analyzed under three separate constitutional doctrines: (1) due process; (2) Fifth Amendment protections against self-incrimination; and (3) Fourth Amendment protections against unreasonable searches and seizures.

Due Process Considerations in Urinalysis

The due process limitation on governmental activity involved in urinalysis affects the nature of the test itself and the procedures employed in conducting such tests. The leading case is *Rochin* v. *California*,[49] in which deputy sheriffs forcibly entered Rochin's room and saw him hurriedly put capsules in his mouth. The officers forcibly attempted to extract the capsules to no avail and then took Rochin to a hospital where at the direction of one of the officers, a doctor forced an emetic solution through a tube into Rochin's stomach against his will causing him to vomit up the capsules. The capsules were introduced at his trial. The Court held that the activities of the officers both in struggling to open his mouth and the subsequent forcible extraction of his stomach's contents offended "even hardened sensibilities" and were thus violative of due process.

Rochin puts a limit on governmental intrusion into a person's bodily integrity. However, subsequent cases have upheld other types of intrusions. In *Breithaupt* v. *Abram*,[50] and *Schmerber* v. *California*[51] the Supreme Court upheld the withdrawal of blood from unconscious and unconsenting drivers. In *Schmerber* the court noted that the extraction "was made by a physician in a simple, medically accepted manner in a hospital environment."

The test remains whether the Court's conscience is shocked by the nature of the intrusion and with *Rochin* and *Schmerber* as guides, it would appear unlikely that compulsory urinalysis testing accomplished by testing voluntarily expelled samples would violate due process.[52] The methods employed to promote involuntary expulsion would have to be evaluated separately. Certainly, forcible use of a catheter or direct removal of urine from the bladder by needle entry through the abdomen, would raise serious due process considerations. Drugs that would cause expulsion without other side effects would be more immune from attack, particularly considering the lower courts' apparent hardening of their sensibilities in recent years, in refusing to apply *Rochin* to a variety of procedures primarily in narcotic cases.[53]

Due process considerations also dictate that tests be conducted in accordance with sound medical practice. Variations from prescribed levels of sanitation and staff expertise that affect the health of the person giving the sample would violate *Rochin*; the same practices would affect the validity of the sampling results, and thus tend to undercut the effectiveness of the identification program.

Fifth Amendment Considerations in Urinalysis

The Fifth Amendment generally prohibits the government from forcing a person to incriminate himself. There is little question that urine sampling does produce information that could be the basis for a criminal prosecution. However, the courts have limited the applicability of the Fifth Amendment to testimonial evidence. In a substantial line of decisions the Supreme Court has indicated that physical evidence including body fluids is not protected by the Fifth Amendment.

The leading case is *Schmerber* v. *California*,[54] where the Court upheld the taking of a blood sample from an unconsenting driver. Regarding the driver's Fifth Amendment claim the court reasoned:

Not even a shadow of testimonial compulsion upon or enforced communication by the accused was involved either in the extraction or in the chemical analysis. Petitioner's testimonial capacities were in no way implicated; indeed, his participation except as a donor, was irrelevant to the results of the test, which depend on chemical analysis and on that alone. Since the blood test evidence, although an incriminating product of compulsion, was neither petitioner's testimony nor evidence relating to some communicative act or writing by the petitioner, it was not inadmissible on privilege grounds.[55]

It should be noted, however, that no court has had occasion to consider an investigatory scheme in which blood or urine sampling is uniformly linked with compulsory interviewing. Where the fruits of a body search are employed exclusively to guide interviewers or to verify interview results, it may be logical to consider the physical search itself as a mere step in the process of obtaining "testimonial" evidence, and to extend the coverage of the Fifth Amendment privilege to all compelled participation in this process.[56]

Fourth Amendment Considerations in Urinalysis

Is Urine Sampling a Search or Seizure? The Fourth Amendment secures citizens against unreasonable searches and seizures and creates the most substantial constitutional hurdle for routine urinalysis conducted on all arrested persons as part of an addict-identification program. It is clear that urine sampling is a "search and seizure" within the meaning of the Fourth Amendment and thus subject to the reasonableness standard. In *Schmerber* v. *California*,[57] the Supreme Court was empathic in holding that the taking of blood samples was a search within the Fourth Amendment:

That Amendment [Fourth] expressly provides that "[t]he right of the people to be secure in their *persons*, houses, papers, and effects, against unreasonable searches and seizures, shall not be violated. . . ." It could not reasonably be argued, and indeed respondent does not argue, that the administration of the blood test in this case was free of the constraints of the Fourth Amendment. Such testing procedures plainly constitute searches of "persons" and depend antecedently upon seizures of "persons" within the meaning of that Amendment.[58]

It has, however, been argued elsewhere that urine sampling is not a search or seizure because the sample is "the result of a natural expulsion function that must occur during incarceration, whether or not for the purpose of urinalysis."[59] The argument proceeds with the apparently rhetorical question: ". . . could it be seriously considered an unreasonable search to initially collect the urine in a specimen jar rather than a toilet facility?"[60]

The Fourth Amendment puts limits on searches and seizures. While it has some surface appeal to consider collection of voluntarily expelled urine not a "search" in the same sense as the involuntarily extracted blood in *Schmerber*, it can hardly be considered something less than a "seizure" for which the same standards are applicable. Furthermore, the Supreme Court has held Fourth Amendment standards applicable in instances where the item seized was voluntarily expelled. In *Katz* v. *United States*,[61] government agents attached an electronic listening and recording device to the outside of a public phone booth and recorded the petitioner's conversations. Those conversations were "voluntarily expelled" but, of course, were hardly undertaken with the expectation or the desire that government agents should sample them. The Court held the agent's actions in violation of the Fourth Amendment. The Court noted: "What a person knowingly exposes to the public, even in his own home or office, is not a subject of Fourth Amendment protection. . . . But what he seeks to preserve as private, even in an area accessible to the public, may be constitutionally protected."[62]

The expulsion of urine has not yet become in contemporary American society a public act. The expectation of privacy that surrounded a public telephone booth in *Katz* surely extends to the jailhouse urinal. In addition, persons confined awaiting trial (for whom the presumption of innocence applies) must be provided with the necessities of life including adequate bathroom facilities. It would appear constitutionally suspect to provide such necessities under the condition that their use might seriously implicate the arrestee in the commission of a crime. At a minimum, the reasonableness standards of the Fourth Amendment would be applicable.

Is the Search or Seizure Reasonable? The Fourth Amendment normally requires that police officers obtain a judicial warrant prior to conducting a search or seizure. The judicial officer is to determine if probable cause exists for the search or seizure. The officer is to indicate specifically the area to be searched and the items to be seized. Any search conducted without a warrant is "per se unreasonable . . .—subject only to a few specifically established and well-delineated exceptions."[63]

The imposition of a warrant requirement would in most instances effectively eliminate routine urine testing of all arrested persons. Where a detainee exhibits no obvious signs or symptoms of drug dependence (and where urinalysis is thus a uniquely valuable addict-identification technique), a warrant based on a sufficient showing of probable cause could not issue. All detainees would not have been arrested for drug offenses and thus the probable cause justifying the initial arrest would not support addict-identification procedures. The time needed to obtain a warrant may also effectively reduce the value of the subsequent test.

The fact that urine sampling and testing would be conducted by other than police officers would not affect the Fourth Amendment's applicability. A search and seizure by any governmental agent is conditioned by the same legal standards whether employed by a police force, a public health organization, or an administrative body.[64] Of course, since the operational language of the Fourth Amendment is the reasonableness of the search, the purpose for which the search is conducted may affect the balancing required in evaluating searches conducted without a warrant. It is then to the "well-delineated exceptions" to the warrant requirements that diversion programmers must turn in efforts to justify routine sampling of all detained persons.

Investigatory Search and Seizure. One of the exceptions to the warrant requirement authorized by the Supreme Court involves the police tactic of "stop and frisk." The Court held that police are authorized to conduct limited searches of suspicious persons on their own initiative in situations where time constraints or the burden of showing probable cause, or both, would make the task of obtaining a warrant impossible.[65] As a general rule, it can be said that in all permissible investigatory searches, two elements must be present: urgency arising from the seriousness of the anticipated danger, and "reasonable cause" in the mind of the officer that focuses attention on the person searched. Although the Supreme Court recently relaxed the standards for evaluating "reasonable cause",[66] it did not intimate that an investigatory search in which the investigator has no special grounds for focusing attention on a particular individual can be countenanced under the Fourth Amendment.[67] Police officers cannot randomly search every individual passing a certain street corner. Yet it is precisely the element of nonselectivity that makes mandatory urinalysis in detention a valuable addict-identification technique. It does not seem likely that the investigatory search doctrine, designed to protect police officers from bodily harm, could be extended to finding traces of drug use.

A case that comes closest to involving the particular problems of addict-identification procedures is *Committee for G.I. Rights* v. *Callaway.*[68] The case challenged the Army's drug-abuse prevention plan, which was designed to identify drug pushers and users, to provide medical assistance, counselling and other rehabilitative measures, and, where rehabilitation failed, to remove confirmed drug users from the service. Soldiers were initially put in the program when they were "suspected" of drug abuse. Suspicion could be supported by what the district court found to be "vague criteria," which in part could be developed by a drug-inspection plan. As the district court described the inspection, it was conducted as follows:

Inspectors are permitted to examine all of the soldiers' property (although they may search personal items such as wallets only cursorily in order to determine the presence of contraband), their clothing and even their entire exterior skin area for drugs or indications of drug use. All inspections are to be conducted without undue harassment, in the presence of those whose property is under examination, and, in the case of skin searches, with as much privacy as is possible. Groin or anal inspections must be conducted by qualified medical personnel in complete privacy.[69]

When a soldier was identified as a drug user, he was subject to mandatory rehabilitative programming. He was medically evaluated to verify drug use and then sent to a center for development of a rehabilitative program that might include urine and other testing, counselling, and treatment. At the end of 60 days the commander determined whether or not the drug abuser was a "rehabilitative success." If not, he was discharged. If he was a success he was returned to normal duties but was subject to unannounced urinalysis testing twice a month. As the district court noted, the "effects of this processing, including preclusion from promotion and the stigma of having been labeled a confirmed drug abuser, may continue long after even the follow-up period has terminated successfully." Facts developed during any stage of the program could be used in court martial trials.

The district court found the Army program violative of constitutional protections including the Fourth Amendment provision against unreasonable searches and seizures. In language particularly applicable to civilian addict-identification programs, it held:

The drug inspection described above constitutes a mass search, and would be illegal in a civilian context if conducted in the absence of particularized probable cause. Moreover, the subsequent use for disciplinary purposes of facts developed during such a search or during participation in a rehabilitative program ordered by reason of an illegal search would be equally improper. The fruits of an initial illegality cannot be used to punish. ... In fact, since the rehabilitative program contemplated by the circular itself entails intrusive searches and interrogation, information obtained during drug processing could not be used for disciplinary purposes unless the Army had probable cause, obtained independently of that processing, to believe that a particular soldier was guilty of drug abuse.[70]

The opinion, however, went on to note:

The difficulty with the circular, as plaintiffs repeatedly point out, is that it attempts to deal with the drug abuse problem not only as a health problem, as Congress intended, but also as a disciplinary problem. The Army has, since 1970, moved gradually in the direction of rehabilitation rather than discipline in dealing with medical problems such as drugs, alcohol, personality disorders, and the like, but it has not foreclosed its punitive options. While the Court can see nothing unreasonable in conducting intrusive searches without probable cause for the sole purpose of placing individuals into a medically oriented drug rehabilitation program, or with placing soldiers merely suspected of drug abuse into such a program, the USAREUR drug plan is not so limited. Far more than reasonable health monitoring precautions are involved. ... Information developed for medical purposes can be used in court martial proceedings, to impose strict administrative sanctions, and to justify an unfavorable discharge which will follow the G.I. for the rest of his life.[71]

The Circuit Court of Appeals for the District of Columbia reversed the district court holding and upheld the Army's drug-treatment program. However, the appellate court emphasized that in doing so it relied on earlier United States Supreme Court decisions recognizing that the "fundamental necessity for obedience and the consequent necessity for imposition of discipline, may render permissible within the military that which would be constitutionally impermissible outside of it.[72] The appellate court in balancing the governmental interest against the privacy interest of the individual soldier found the governmental interest predominant and the search reasonable because of the totality of five factors: (1) drug abuse poses a substantial threat to the "readiness and efficiency of our military forces"; (2) the soldier's expectation of privacy is different from a civilian's; (3) the "primary purpose" of the program was regulatory not punitive; (4) the program as implemented was the most "effective means of identifying drug users"; and (5) the program attempted to "guard the dignity and privacy of the soldier insofar as practical."[73]

The Army program considered in *Callaway* bears a close resemblance to features of some addict-diversion programs in civilian life. The major thrust of both is medically to treat drug addiction; in both, nonselective search procedures are employed to identify persons for treatment; in both, the persons subject to the program are of a status that traditionally has been subjected to a lessening of constitutional standards regarding governmental intrusion. The critical factor to the district court was that information obtained during a rehabilitative program could be used to impose adverse consequences on persons participating. The list of adverse consequences included sanctions short of criminal conviction. In the pretrial addict-diversion program, the potential for adverse consequences exists. While being identified may qualify an individual for diversion, it may also have the effect of conditioning his release prior to trial in ways not applicable to nondrug users. The fact of drug use may well be employed by judges at sentencing. And, of course, a finding as to the fact of drug use may provide a lead to further prosecution for drug-related offenses. In determining the reasonableness of the search, the potential harm to the person searched would be one important factor, and the confidentiality of the information obtained would determine the scope of the potential harm. The problems of maintaining the confidentiality of treatment information is considered elsewhere.

The force of the *Callaway* decision for purposes of evaluating the legality of procedures in civilian addict-diversion programs is uncertain. The lower court opinion raises substantial questions about the validity of some drug addict-identification procedures and even in reversing the lower court, the circuit court was careful to restrict its holding to a military environment. An argument can be constructed that military authorities have a greater interest in detecting drug addiction than jail officials. Many soldiers are in sensitive positions involving not only the national security of the United States but also its political relations with other countries. Soldiers are in control of weapons of varying destructive capacities. Pretrial detainees, on the other hand, are not depended upon by society; rather, they are dependent upon their keepers. While incarcerated they can do little damage to society itself. The interest in isolating drug users in this class is far less substantial than in the military. One suspects the courts would not find constitutionally permissible a program that, while abolishing all criminal or other sanctions, proceeded to force every person passing a certain intersection to be subjected to a strip search and urinalysis. Little of substance separates pretrial detainees from free citizens when the governmental interest in addict identification is considered. And even while the expectation of privacy of a detainee may be less than that of a free citizen, the expectation results more from the shabby way in which persons accused of criminal acts have been and continue to be treated than from any constitutionally acceptable premise.

The activities of government agents at borders, and the recent cases involving security devices at airports involve circumstances of generalized searches without warrants. However, neither group of cases fairly supports routine urine sampling of all detainees. It has generally been held that routine searches at borders are permissible without a warrant. However, in its most recent decision, the Supreme Court recognized that authorized border searches were limited to those conducted at the border or its equivalent and invalidated a search conducted 25 miles from the border.[74] Thus, the extent to which the federal interest in protecting its borders justifies routine, nonselective searches was severely limited. The case demonstrates the care with which exceptions to the warrant requirement of the Fourth Amendment are framed. In a number of the border search cases in lower courts, extensive searches of personal effects and persons have been invalidated where there was not some reasonable suspicion to single out the individual searched.[75] It does not seem probable that the courts will equate the interest of the government in conducting routine border searches with the interest of the government in addict diversion. Travel across an international border is a consensual act where persons recognize the tradition of routine but nonintrusive searches of person and effects. The expectation of complete privacy is largely absent. There can hardly be implied consent to urinalysis in the context of pretrial detention.

The recent case law arising out of the peculiar context of airport anti-hijacking measures suggests that where an urgent generalized threat of danger to persons is sufficiently extreme, individualized grounds for "reasonable cause" as to each individual searched is not required.[76] However, even in this context some courts have limited the right to search without particularized probable cause. The New York Court of Appeals has held that use of a magnetometer for predeparture searches is a reasonable search but that the triggering of the device did not automatically justify further action other than precluding the passenger from boarding.[77] The court suggested that further search, absent consent, would violate the Fourth Amendment. To extrapolate from the context of airport searches (an area so heavily overlaid with consent issues) to the mandatory urinalysis of persons detained following arrest is to unduly stretch the meaning of the airport cases.

Searches Incident to Arrest. Another exception to the rule that a warrant is required prior to a search involves police activity subsequent to a lawful arrest. It is generally agreed that officers may search the person and effects of an individual lawfully arrested.[78] The scope of such a search, however, is not as yet well defined. And, in evaluating the applicability of such cases to urinalysis for addict-identification purposes, one has to consider two separate contexts in which searches incident to arrest can occur. The first and most frequent cases involve searches conducted immediately upon arrest for the primary purpose of detecting weapons and evidence. The second set of cases involve the procedures employed at detention facilities as a routine matter, the justification for which arises out of the needs of jail security and prisoner identification. Neither set of cases provide support for routine, nonselective urine sampling of pretrial detainees.

The authority for police to search incident to arrest without a warrant is of long standing. In one of the major cases, the Supreme Court articulated the rationale for the exception in the following language:

When an arrest is made, it is reasonable for the arresting officer to search the person arrested in order to remove any weapons that the latter might seek to use in order to resist arrest or effect his escape. Otherwise, the officer's safety might well be endangered, and the arrest itself frustrated. In addition, it is entirely reasonable for the arresting officer to search for and seize any evidence on the arrestee's person in order to prevent its concealment or destruction.[79]

The circumstances under which such searches can be conducted were greatly expanded in the recent decision of *United States* v. *Robinson.*[80] The petitioner was arrested upon probable cause that he was operating an automobile without a license. During a subsequent search, an external patdown, the officer felt an object in petitioner's pocket. It turned out to be a crumpled cigarette pack containing capsules of heroin. The Supreme Court, in a 6–3 decision, upheld the search as incident to the lawful custodial arrest of the petitioner. The petitioner had argued that there was no factual basis from which the officer could have deduced that a search for evidence or weapons would be productive. The Court in rejecting the contention held:

The authority to search the person incident to a lawful custodial arrest, while based upon the need to disarm and to discover evidence, does not depend on what a court may later decide was the probability in a particular arrest situation that weapons or evidence would in fact be found upon the person of the suspect. A custodial arrest of a suspect based on probable cause is a reasonable intrusion under the Fourth Amendment; that intrusion being lawful, a search incident to the arrest requires no additional justification.[81]

At least one state supreme court has refused to follow *Robinson.*[82]

While the Court appears, at first blush, to authorize all searches subsequent to a lawful custodial arrest, routine urine samples of all arrestees is a search far removed from the issue confronting the Court in *Robinson.* The Court continued to recognize that the search incident to arrest doctrine is based on the need to preserve evidence and to discover weapons. In *Robinson* the Court decreed that every custodial arrest will justify a search of this kind; no *additional* showing is required that evidence is likely to be destroyed or that a weapon is likely to exist. The Court emphasized the fact that in custodial arrest the officer's decision to search is "necessarily a quick ad hoc judgment" that ought not be subject to prior review in the courts.

The preservation of evidence and the check for weapons are not even tangentially involved in the routine urine sampling of all arrested persons. In fact, in all likelihood, the search incident to the arrest has already taken place. The decision to search is not a "quick ad hoc judgment" but a studied procedure routinely engaged in to identify addicts. The intrusion of arrest has little relation to the subsequent seizure of the urine sample.

The case most closely analogous to routine urine sampling is again *Schmerber* v. *California*,[83] in which the Supreme Court authorized a blood-alcohol test on an unconsenting motorist. The Court noted that the outward characteristics and actions of the driver provided probable cause to arrest him for drunk driving and these same actions justified taking the blood sample. The Court noted that a warrant requirement would interfere with the test because the time to obtain the warrant would alter the validity of the test. The Court, however, limited its holding as follows:

The interests in human dignity and privacy which the Fourth Amendment protects forbid any such intrusions on the mere chance that desired evidence might be obtained. In the absence of a clear indication that in fact such evidence will be found, these fundamental human interests require law officers to suffer the risk that such evidence may disappear unless there is an immediate search.[84]

Thus, after *Schmerber* it would appear that only those individuals properly arrested for drug-related offenses or evidencing outward manifestations of drug use could be compelled to undergo urinalysis. Large-scale testing of all pretrial detainees would not fit within the incident to arrest exception articulated in *Schmerber*.

Another facet of searches incident to arrest and detention involve the routine booking procedures and activities necessary as an incident to operation of a detention facility. Historically, it was by no means clear that a person in custody following arrest, by virtue of the fact of his detention, could be made subject to examinations that would violate the Fourth Amendment rights of free men. Fifty years ago, the New York courts held that merely fingerprinting a detainee over his protest amounted to an impermissible invasion of his privacy.[85] Today, however, it appears settled that while a pretrial detainee does not check his constitutional rights at the jailhouse door, his keepers are nevertheless authorized to make significant inroads on his privacy in the interest of promoting efficient law enforcement and proper regulation of the detention facility. Over his protests, a detainee can be fingerprinted, photographed, and measured.[86] He can apparently also be required to display his physical characteristics at investigatory lineups, even in connection with pending open cases that are not directly related to the charge on which he is being held.[87] Periodic general shakedown searches for weapons and contraband are also apparently still within the competence of jail authorities although there are those who have questioned the unbridled power to conduct such searches absent some judicial controls.[88] A difficult case, arguably analogous to routine urine testing, would be the routine testing of detainees for communicable diseases. No reported case has been found in which a rationally conceived and humanely administered program of diagnostic testing in detention has been challenged; it is assumed, however, that the compelling need of jail authorities to prevent the spread of smallpox, tuberculosis, and other active contagious diseases within their institutions would justify such testing.[89] At the same time, it should be noted that while drug dependence is often termed a communicable disease for purposes of official rhetoric, it is not contagious in the strict clinical sense; moreover, the environment of a secure, drug-free custodial institution is not conducive to its transmission by example, association, or inducement.

A recent Supreme Court decision provides some guidance in evaluating the scope of pretrial detention searches. In *United States* v. *Edwards*,[90] the petitioner was lawfully arrested and placed in the city jail charged with attempted breaking into a post office. The following morning, ten hours after the arrest, officials brought substitute clothing for the petitioner and seized that which he was wearing. The clothing, containing paint particles matching those of the post office, was introduced into evidence. The Court upheld the search as consistent with Fourth Amendment principles. The court of appeals had invalidated the search on the basis that the "administrative process and the mechanics of the arrest" had ended, and thus the incident to arrest exception for warrantless searches would not be applicable. The Supreme Court reversed, in a 5–4 decision written by Justice White. The majority opinion held:

> . . . once the defendant is lawfully arrested and is in custody, the effects in his possession at the place of detention that were subject to search at the time and place of his arrest may lawfully be searched and seized without a warrant even though a substantial period of time has elapsed between the arrest and subsequent administrative processing on the one hand and the taking of the property for use as evidence on the other. This is true where the clothing or effects are immediately seized upon arrival at the jail, held under the defendant's name in the "property room" of the jail, and at a later time searched and taken for use at the subsequent criminal trial. The result is the same where the property is not physically taken from the defendant until some time after his incarceration.[91]

This language might be thought to support the taking of a urine sample as one of the "effects" the person arrested has in his possession at the time of arrest. However, the majority opinion casts serious doubt on whether *Edwards* can be read that broadly. In footnote 9 of the opinion the majority concludes first that the warrant requirement of the Fourth Amendment may still be applicable to some custodial searches and then indicates that the Court "has no occasion to express a view concerning those circumstances surrounding custodial searches incident to incarceration which might 'violate the dictates of reason either because of their number or their manner of perpetration.' " Cited immediately thereafter is *Schmerber* v. *California*. It thus seems that at least to Justice White, a situation like *Schmerber* requires either probable cause or a warrant. If blood is not a personal effect subject to a warrantless search incident to arrest it would appear urine should be similarly treated.

The dissenting opinion in *Edwards* written by Justice Stewart and concurred in by Justices Douglas, Brennan, and Marshall call attention to a distinction regarding the purpose of a search in the jail context. In footnote 2 of his opinion, Justice Stewart indicates the government conceded the seizure of the clothing was not a matter of routine jail procedure. He continued:

No contention is made that the warrantless seizure of the clothes was necessitated by the exigencies of maintaining discipline or security within the jail system. There is thus no occasion to consider the legitimacy of warrantless searches or seizure in an institution based upon that quite different rationale.[92]

It appears clear that neither the majority nor the four dissenters viewed *Edwards* as involving the same type of interests that would arguably be present in an addict-identification procedure. The applicability of the Fourth Amendment even to those procedures based on "maintaining discipline or security within the jail system" appear unresolved. The interest in such searches is considerably more immediate and compelling than the interests advanced by routine and nonselective sampling of detainees' urine.

It does not appear that administrative necessity and jail security could be forcefully advanced to justify compulsory urine sampling for addict identification. It is first clear that unjustifiably intrusive or indiscriminate searches at pretrial detention intake are violations of constitutional rights.[93] In order to justify mandatory urinalysis screening or pretrial detainees, it would be necessary to assert that addict identification is essential to anticipate the treatment needs of prisoners who later may suffer drug-withdrawal symptoms, and thus threaten institutional security, or that the identification of drug-dependent pretrial detainees is a necessary step in enforcing institutional rules against drug-contraband traffic.[94] Neither argument seems likely to succeed since both interests can be adequately secured by means that do not involve intrusive and indiscriminate search procedures. Withdrawal is properly treated only after its symptoms appear, and since inmates suffering those symptoms will either be readily identifiable by jail personnel or will identify themselves by requesting medication, early identification is a medical convenience at most. Contraband drug trafficking is a general problem in pretrial-detention populations, which can be most effectively controlled by securing infirmary drug supplies and screening all transactions with the community. Thus, the administrative importance of urinalysis data is open to question.[95] It should be noted also that only a minority of arrestees tested during prearraignment detention will ultimately be jailed for any length of time; as to those arrestees who will not be held in custody pending trial, medical and security justifications for mandatory urinalysis are wholly inapplicable.

Existing case law does not deal directly with the problem presented in mandatory urine sampling. Whether such a program can be justified as one "incident to arrest" is not definitively determined. However, the rationale thus far advanced for warrantless searches incident to lawful arrests does not support such sampling programs. For the courts to validate such a procedure would require them to indicate a new interest that would justify extending the exception to the Fourth Amendment. Whether the interest in addict identification and treatment supports such an extension is considered in a subsequent section.[96]

Administrative Searches. An area that has given the United States Supreme Court great difficulty is where governmental officials seek to search premises for what are primarily administrative purposes but which can lead to criminal prosecutions. In *Frank* v. *Maryland*,[97] the Court held that a warrantless search by a municipal health inspector was not a violation of the Fourth Amendment and that a criminal conviction for refusing to allow the search was constitutional. The decision was 5–4 but was thought to validate administrative inspection searches where the primary purpose was regulatory rather than criminal and the public interest was such as to justify the search.

However, in two subsequent cases, *Camara* v. *Municipal Court of the City and County of San Francisco*,[98] and *See* v. *City of Seattle*,[99] the Court specifically overruled *Frank* v. *Maryland* and held that administrative searches were subject to a warrant requirement. The *Camara* case involved a criminal conviction for refusing to allow city housing inspectors to conduct a warrantless inspection of a home for violations of the building codes. In *See* the appellant was convicted of refusing to allow city fire inspectors to inspect his commercial warehouse as part of a routine, periodic citywide canvass to obtain compliance with a city fire code. While the Supreme Court declined to allow municipalities to dispense with the warrant procedure in such inspections, it did indicate that judicial authorization to enter the property of a nonconsenting building owner could be based on a showing of less than specific probable cause and could be conducted on an areawide basis. As Justice White indicated for the majority:

Having concluded that the area inspection is a "reasonable" search of private property within the meaning of the Fourth Amendment, it is obvious that "probable cause" to issue a warrant to inspect must exist if reasonable legislative or administrative standards for conducting an area inspection are satisfied with respect to a particular dwelling. Such standards, which will vary with the municipal program being enforced, may be based upon the passage of time, the nature of the building (e.g., a multi-family apartment house), or the condition of the entire area, but they will not necessarily depend upon specific knowledge of the condition of the particular dwelling.[100]

The full scope of the *Camara* and *See* cases remains unresolved. In a subsequent case, the Court authorized a warrantless inspection of a federally licensed gun dealer on the basis that a statute authorized the inspection and the extent of federal regulation of licensees justified the inspection involved.[101] In another case the Court noted that the government could constitutionally deny ADC benefits to persons who would not permit welfare workers to enter their homes.[102] Thus, there are administrative searches that can be conducted without any warrant whatsoever, and there are administrative searches that can be conducted with a broad judicial warrant based on a generalized rather than a particularized probable cause. It is possible to argue that either set of cases is analogous to nonselective urine sampling of pretrial detainees.

The Business Regulation Cases—No Warrant Required. In *United States* v. *Biswell*,[103] the Supreme Court upheld a statute authorizing warrantless inspection of federally licensed gun dealers. The Court found the search "reasonable" and thus an exception to the Fourth Amendment warrant requirement. Justice White, writing for the majority, recognized two justifications for the result. First, the governmental interest in the regulation of guns is substantial and inspection is an essential and integral part of such regulation. Furthermore:

. . . if inspection is to be effective and serve as a credible deterrent, unannounced, even frequent, inspections are essential. In this context, the prerequisite of a warrant could easily frustrate inspection; and if the necessary flexibility as to time, scope, and frequency is to be preserved, the protections afforded by a warrant would be negligible.[104]

See v. *City of Seattle* was distinguished in that the time delay in securing a warrant would not frustrate the inspection since building conditions could not be easily concealed or corrected.

In balancing this substantial governmental interest in warrantless inspection against the interest in privacy of the gun dealer, Justice White had no difficulty in finding the search "reasonable":

[These inspections] pose only limited threats to the dealer's justifiable expectations of privacy. When a dealer chooses to engage in this pervasively regulated business and to accept a federal license, he does so with the knowledge that his business records, firearms, and ammunition will be subject to inspection. The dealer is not left to wonder about the purposes of the inspector or the limits of his task.[105]

The factors required to be balanced in addict-identification procedures are distinguishable from those the Court dealt with in *Biswell*. First, the Court has long recognized that businesses subject to substantial regulation for health or safety purposes are subject to warrantless inspections.[106] And in *Biswell* the Court relied heavily on suggestions in a case involving the search of liquor dealers where the history of substantial regulation was long standing.[107] While the regulation of drugs is substantial, inspection of a pharmacy is more analogous to *Biswell* than inspection of all persons arrested for crime. Regulation of a business is far different from regulation of human conduct and the distinction has often had constitutional significance.[108]

In addition, the consensual factors in *Biswell* are completely lacking in addict identification. The gun dealer, as the court notes, knows what he is getting into. A person arrested for shoplifting hardly knows or consents to urinalysis. Furthermore, the invasion of privacy is substantially greater than in *Biswell*. *Biswell* involves search of a business establishment open to the public. Urinalysis involves the search of a person. In short, it is doubtful that warrantless search cases involving business regulation support routine urine sampling of pretrial detainees.

Camara and See—A General Warrant. While *Camara* and *See* do not authorize completely warrantless searches, a nonparticularized probable cause requirement for a judicial order would be a middle ground upon which addict identification could proceed. The rationale of these cases might be advanced to justify a procedure under which warrants to conduct urinalysis of detainees who refuse voluntary participation could be sought on a routine basis with a minimal showing of individualized probable cause.

The state interest in identifying drug-dependent persons is arguably as great or greater than its interest in locating structures that may pose dangers to public health or safety, and existing documentation indicates that in many urban jurisdictions the rate of drug dependence among detainees is far higher than the rate for the general population.[109] Significant problems arise, however, in an attempt to extend the *Camara* rationale to addict identification. In *Camara* the extent of the intrusion, that is, into buildings, was far less than searches of persons occasioned by testing urine, particularly where the expulsion of urine is compelled. While the public motive behind addict identification is nonprosecutorial, as was the case in *Camara*, addict diversion is much more a part of criminal procedure and involves governmental authorities much closer to the prosecution than inspectors for building code violations.

It appears unlikely that the majority in *Camara* considered that their holding would be applicable to searches of persons. Since pretrial detainees are protected by the presumption of innocence, extension of generalized warrants to cover such detainees as a class would be very close to similar warrants issued to allow dragnet operations on the public-at-large.[110] While a building may be considered in a class with the neighborhood in which it sits, it is far different to classify people on the basis of a status that might statistically have some merit but that inevitably includes individuals not properly within the class sought, that is, drug users. A different analysis would leave much of the policy behind the Fourth Amendment in jeopardy and would seriously abridge the Warrant Clause and the requirement of showing probable cause.

What Is The Government's Interest? Any interpretation of the Fourth Amendment involves the concept of reasonableness and thus necessarily requires the courts to balance the needs of the government against the intrusion of privacy suffered by individuals. In the previous discussion of exceptions to the Warrant Clause, it has been suggested that the interests in addict diversion are not similar to those found by the Court in prior cases to support warrantless searches. The question remaining open, however, is whether the identification of drug addicts creates a new governmental interest sufficient in the context of diversion programs to justify the nature of the intrusion required for urine testing. The single precedent directly applicable suggests that the governmental interest in military preparedness is sufficient to justify an overriding of the privacy interests of individual soldiers.[111]

The primary interest of diversion-program identification procedures is to identify addicts in order to provide treatment as an alternative to regular processing through the criminal courts. It is thus important to determine the weight to be accorded to the government interest in compelling persons detained awaiting trial to be identified as proper treatment clients.

In the context of pretrial detention it must first be recognized that individuals in the class concerned have not been convicted of any crime. The class contains both persons guilty of the offense charged and persons innocent of any criminal conduct. While the treatment of persons awaiting trial has often ignored the presumption of innocence, courts have increasingly recognized that the decision of a police officer to arrest is insufficient to alter significantly a person's constitutional rights. Courts have held that unconvicted persons have a constitutional right to avoid involuntarily imposed treatment.[112] The interest of identifying drug users in the class of pretrial detainees is thus no greater than the governmental interest in identifying drug users in the general population. Public concern about drug abuse is high and measures to identify drug users are clearly supportable under the police power. But, such interests are of no greater weight than society's interest in detecting individuals who have committed or are committing other crimes. And that interest has never been considered sufficient to outweigh the Fourth Amendment entitlement to privacy.[113] Indeed, the Fourth Amendment was specifically designed to limit society's quest for criminal offenders to methods that did not intrude on an individual's privacy.

The question then should be whether compulsory urine testing is constitutionally sound in a free society. It could be argued that a series of cases upholding compulsory smallpox vaccination,[114] health quarantine,[115] destruction of tubercular cattle,[116] and seizure of unwholesome food[117] support such a program.[118] In *Camara* the majority opinion specifically recognizes the need for such prompt inspections that have "traditionally [been] upheld in emergency situations."[119] It is, however, unlikely that such cases offer much support. Drug addiction is certainly not contagious in the same manner as smallpox. While, of course, it could be argued that the nature of the cycle of use, addiction, and sale has impact on others who might avoid drug use, a similar argument, albeit not as strong, can be made for other criminal offenders. And smallpox can, of course, be transmitted to the totally innocent, whereas the transmission of drug use requires a criminal act by the party to whom the activity is transferred. The distinction is more of kind than of degree. While tempting in this time of concern over increasing drug use, the abrogation of the protections of the Fourth Amendment hardly seems justified in this instance.

A Question of Remedy—Or So What? It is suggested in the above discussion that grave doubts exist about the constitutionality of compulsory nonselective urine sampling of pretrial detainees. The most frequent remedy, however, in instances where the Fourth Amendment has been violated is to preclude the use of illegally seized evidence at a subsequent criminal proceeding. Since diversion staff envision that the results of their testing will not be used for prosecution purposes in any event, it can be argued that the Fourth Amendment problems become theoretical. The exclusionary rule only sanctions unconstitutional methods that lead to criminal proceedings. Such a position is suggested if not advanced in the Special Action Office booklet analyzing the legality of drug-diversion programs:

The TASC samples are not taken for prosecution purposes and would rarely, if ever, be used for prosecution. Thus, there would be little opportunity to raise a challenge and, even if challenged, the exclusionary rule would be of little avail.[120]

The argument has serious overtones. It is surely not an acceptable position for the government that the constitutional rights of its citizens can be systematically violated because remedies are unavailable or ineffective. Nor is it certain that any prosecutor would willingly authorize a procedure he knows will preclude use in a criminal prosecution of information obtained. The existence of such a procedure, even if the actual information obtained was not used, would put subsequent prosecutions under a heavy burden to show that the "fruits" of such information were not used as well.

Of course, an additional answer is that remedies other than application of the exclusionary rule are available. Officials who violate an individual's civil rights are subject to civil damages under the Civil Rights Acts and directly under the Fourth Amendment.[121] And it is possible to obtain an injunction against the systematic violation of Fourth Amendment rights.[122]

Voluntary Consent to Identification Procedures

Constitutional rights are, of course, subject to waiver, and the constitutional objections to addict-identification procedures as discussed above become inapplicable where it can be shown that arrested individuals submit to urinalysis and drug interviews as true volunteers. If, by contrast, current identification procedures are structured to exert coercive pressure toward participation, to conceal from arrestees the existence of their rights to decline, or to provide potential participants misleading or incomplete advice as to the consequences that may flow from consent, they are subject to constitutional challenge. The issues involved in determining whether a waiver is "voluntary" are not unfamiliar to students of criminal procedure, and no attempt to extensively review the applicable case law will be offered. However, some thoughts about the particular applicability of consent doctrines to addict diversion may be useful.

Drug Interviews and Consent

As indicated above,[123] drug-use interviews involve application of the Fifth Amendment privilege against self-incrimination and are thus directly analogous to the cases involving coerced confessions and custodial interrogation by police officers. The issue of whether such interviews involve the possibility of incrimination is considered elsewhere.[124] Courts have traditionally viewed interrogations in a custodial setting as inherently coercive and in *Miranda* v. *Arizona*[125] the Supreme Court provided that prior to such interrogation an individual must be informed of his right to decline to be interviewed, of the potentially damaging uses to which disclosures could be made, and of his right to the assistance of an attorney, to be court appointed if necessary. The application of the *Miranda* doctrine to drug-use interviews seems clear. The scope of its application and the specific effect it will have on current practice remains ambiguous.[126]

Although the primary purpose of addict-identification interviewing is nonprosecutorial, the risk of practical self-incrimination is nevertheless substantial for the individual defendant. And although the interviewers are not generally police officers, the setting in which interviewing occurs is custodial. In the hours immediately after entering custody, the arrestee is poorly situated to appreciate fine distinctions between the mandate of law enforcement personnel and that of the staff of a diversion program; he is likely to regard both groups primarily as representatives of legal authority. The possibility for confusion in such a situation is high. Even assuming that sufficient immunity exists for the conducting of drug interviews, such immunity would not extend, unless expressly so applied, to information given to police officers not associated with the diversion program. But the accused remains in a single custodial setting subject to the questions of both sets of governmental agents. The confusion regarding the incriminatory effect of statements to each, the potential for intentional as well as unintentional deception, and the coerciveness of custody itself would make the policies underlying *Miranda* even more compelling.

The essentially beneficent goals of addict identification, in the context of a diversion program, cannot insulate this form of interrogation from the protections offered in *Miranda*. Police interviews may sometimes be conducted with the benign purpose of assisting the suspect. The chance of incrimination, not the intent of the interviewer, should control.

Whether the constitutional requirement that steps be taken to neutralize the inherent coercive force of custodial interrogation requires that a separate set of *Miranda*-type warnings be given at the outset of each attempt at drug-history interviewing is an open question if the subject has already been given standard *Miranda* warnings upon arrest. If there is a substantial delay between arrest and drug-use interview, the use of some form of "refresher" warning is clearly desirable. This is particularly true since the interviewer will normally represent his intentions to the arrestee as nonprosecutorial, and the arrestee may not appreciate the continuing applicability of a prior *Miranda* warning to this new circumstance.

Urinalysis and Consent

The taking of a urine sample involves application of the Fourth Amendment prohibition against unreasonable searches and seizures. Defining "consent" in the context of the Fourth Amendment has been markedly different from the procedural protections involving the Fifth Amendment illustrated by *Miranda.* Courts have generally not required a warning prior to a search similar to that required prior to interrogation. In *Schneckloth* v. *Bustamonte* the Supreme Court indicated that the voluntariness of the consent must be determined by consideration of a variety of factors.[127] The Court specifically refused to fashion a rule requiring the searching officer to warn the person to be searched of his right to refuse. The Court held that while the prosecution had to prove that the consent was voluntary, it did not have to meet the greater burden of showing it was a knowing and intelligent waiver of a Fourth Amendment right, the latter standard being reserved for rights directly affecting the criminal trial. The Court noted that the Fourth Amendment protects privacy, not the fairness of the trial itself. A careful reading of *Schneckloth*, however, places its applicability to addict identification procedures in some doubt.

In *Schneckloth*, the officer stopped an automobile that was missing a headlight. Six men were in the automobile. When only one could produce identification, the officer asked if he could search the automobile and was given permission. The search uncovered checks stolen in an earlier burglary, which were admitted at the trial. Arguing that the officer did not inform them of their rights to refuse the search, the defendants sought to have the checks excluded. The Supreme Court found, 6–3, that the consent was voluntary.

In distinguishing the search cases from custodial interrogation cases such as *Miranda*, Justice Stewart writing for the majority indicated that it would be "thoroughly impractical to impose on the normal consent search, the detailed requirements of an effective warning."[128] The "normal consent search" occurs on the highway or at a person's home in an "informal and unstructured" setting.[129] The search may be a logical extension of police interrogation, and the circumstances suggesting the search may arise quickly.[130] In this context, the majority saw a warning requirement as unduly burdensome. However, addict-identification procedures take place under entirely different circumstances. Urinalysis takes place in the highly structured custodial setting of the police station or detention facility and is part of a planned program of identification. A warning is easily included as a component of that procedure.

Schneckloth may, in fact, not be applicable to custodial searches. Justice Stewart expressly noted that the situation of the normal consent search is "still immeasurably far removed" from the custodial interrogation involved in *Miranda*.[131] And in footnote 29 of the opinion, the Court clearly stated that the case "does not require a determination of the proper standard to be applied in assessing the validity of a search authorized solely by an alleged consent that is obtained from a person after he has been placed in custody."[132] The Court there also cites cases where courts have been "particularly sensitive to the heightened possibilities for coercion" in custodial settings. Among them is *Judd* v. *United States*,[133] where the court invalidated a search conducted of an accused's home where consent had been obtained while the accused was in jail. The court noted:

This burden on the Government is particularly heavy in cases where the individual is under arrest. Non-resistance to the orders or suggestions of the police is not infrequent in such a situation, true consent, free of fear or pressure, is not so readily to be found. ... In fact, the circumstances of the defendant's plight may be such as to make any claim of actual consent "not in accordance with human experience" and explainable only on the basis of "physical or moral compulsion."[134]

On the other hand, the circuit courts that have confronted the issue have held that *Schneckloth* is fully applicable to consent searches where the consent is obtained while the accused is in custody.[135] However, these same courts have recognized that the fact of custody is a critical factor in evaluating the voluntariness of the search. And perhaps even more directly applicable to diversion programs, a federal district court in New York invalidated a consent search pursuant to a signed waiver required of all persons admitted to parole. The court after acknowledging *Schneckloth* went on to hold: "Only Coleman's signature on a dotted line could secure the benefit of parole. A refusal to sign slammed the cell door shut until January 1977, more than eight years.... Under these circumstances, I find sufficient coercion present to invalidate the consent to search executed."[136]

Conditioning access to diversion programs with a requirement that the participant consent to a search poses a similar choice between trial with possible imprisonment or search with possible release.

In the Fifth Amendment area, the Court resolved the problem of consent by requiring the *Miranda* warnings and a standard that required the prosecution to prove that his Fifth Amendment rights were "intelligently and knowingly waived." *Schneckloth*, while rejecting such a ruling in the noncustodial consent search cases, does not preclude the applicability of the greater standard to consent obtained in custody. Thus, it may be required that diversion staff specifically advise detainees that they may refuse to authorize a urine sample and test.

Notes

1. Most addict-diversion programs are presently designed for heroin addicts, a drug for which urinalysis is a relatively reliable identification procedure. However, in evaluating the legality of these procedures it is

important to recognize that programs directed toward users of other drugs may require different and less reliable testing methods.

2. Some programs may use physicians or psychiatrists as screeners. See MASS. GEN. LAWS. ANN. ch. 123 § 47 (Supp. 1974) requiring an evaluation by a psychiatrist or physician. This may raise problems of patient–physician privilege. The Massachusetts program is voluntary. See generally, Robertson, *Pre-trial Diversion of Drug Offenders: A Statutory Approach*, 52 B.U.L. REV. 335 (1972).

3. A recent study of the utility of mass urinalysis screening in the Philadelphia TASC project suggests that such a procedure may not be necessary. The study found that self-admission of narcotics use was the most useful indicator. The study concluded: "Were the urinalysis results able to either identify significant numbers of narcotics involved arrestees not identified by other methods, or were they able to discriminate on salient variables in groups of arrestees, then a case could have been made for retention of the procedure. Since neither of these decision making relevant outcomes was demonstrated to be the case, elimination of the mass urinalysis screening was indicated." LEAA, TASC TALK (December 1974).

4. The validity of such assurances is subject to question. See page 15, *infra.*

5. Robinson v. California, 370 U.S. 660 (1962).

6. *See, e.g.*, ICC v. Brimson, 154 U.S. 447 (1894) (proceeding of regulatory agencies); Quinn v. United States, 349 U.S. 155 (1955) (congressional committee investigations).

7. United States v. Sullivan, 274 U.S. 259 (1927) (income tax return can be compelled even though accurate statement of income would disclose illegal activities).

8. 382 U.S. 70 (1965).

9. 390 U.S. 39 (1968).

10. Grosso v. United States, 390 U.S. 62 (1968); Haynes v. United States 390 U.S. 85 (1968).

11. Marchetti v. United States, 390 U.S. 29, 54 (1968).

12. 402 U.S. 424 (1971).

13. *Id.* at 454.

14. Meltzer, *Privileges Against Self-Incrimination and the Hit-and-Run Opinions*, 1971 SUP. CT. REV. 1.

15. 21 U.S.C. § 1175 (1974). See discussion of this section at page 98, *infra.*

16. In the mental examination context the available sanctions for noncooperation range from contempt to the requirement that a plea of not

guilty by reason of insanity be withdrawn. The indigent defendant is in a more difficult position since state-underwritten expert testimony on his mental state may be the only such testimony practically available. *See* Note, *Pretrial Psychiatric Examinations and the Privilege Against Self-Incrimination,* 1971 U. I.LL. L. F. 232,243–44.

17. United States v. Albright, 388 F.2d 719 (4th Cir. 1968); Taylor v. United States, 222 F.2d 398 (D.C. Cir. 1955).

18. Special Action Office for Drug Abuse Prevention, TASC Legal Analysis, Part III, at 29 (Sept. 1973) (hereinafter referred to as TASC Legal Analysis). The analysis was issued by the Special Action Office and was based on material prepared under grants to Lewis and Clark College, Northwestern School of Law and Wayne State University. The study refers to 21 U.S.C. § 1175 as a potential immunity provision. It is doubtful however whether the statute, given its express exceptions, would withstand scrutiny as the type of statute necessary to obviate Fifth Amendment objections. *See* page 15, *infra.*

19. The Philadelphia study of addict-identification techniques, *supra* note 3, indicates that self-admission is the most useful factor in identifying potential diversion clients.

20. Hamilton v. Love, 328 F.2d 1182 (E.D. Ark. 1971).

21. *See, e.g.,* State v. Whitlow, 45 N.J. 3, 210 A.2d 763 (1965).

22. *See, e.g.,* State v. Ruskin, 34 Wis.2d 607, 150 N.W.2d 318 (1967); Note, *Changing Standards for Compulsory Mental Examinations,* 1969 WIS. L. REV. 270 (1969).

23. *See, e.g.,* United States v. Williams, 456 F.2d 217 (5th Cir. 1972); United States v. Bohle, 445 F.2d 54 (7th Cir. 1971); United States v. Albright, 388 F.2d 719 (4th Cir. 1968).

24. Note, *supra* note 16 at 235-37.

25. *See, e.g.,* United States v. Albright, *supra* note 17.

26. 250 Ore. 288, 442 P.2d 238 (1968).

27. 250 Ore. at 293–94, 442 P.2d at 241.

28. United States v. Albright, *supra* note 17, at 724.

29. Hoffman v. United States, 341 U.S. 479 (1951).

30. Kastigar v. United States, 406 U.S. 441 (1972); Zicarelli v. New Jersey State Commission of Investigation, 406 U.S. 472 (1972).

31. Kastigar v. United States, 406 U.S. at 460 (1972).

32. Counselman v. Hitchcock, 142 U.S. 547 (1892).

33. *Supra* note 31.

34. 18 U.S.C. § 6002 (1970).

35. Zicarelli v. New Jersey State Commission of Investigation, *supra* note 30, at 475.

36. 21 U.S.C. § 1175 (Supp. 1974).

37. The original statutory language read "authorized or assisted under any provision of this Act." Initially interpretive regulations construed the statute narrowly to include only programs actually conducted by the United States. 37 Fed. Reg. 24636, 24637 (Nov. 17, 1972). This was expanded in subsequent regulations to those programs "supported" by an agency of the United States. 38 Fed. Reg. 33746 (Dec. 6, 1973). Current regulations interpret "indirectly assisted" to include programs funded by general revenue sharing funds or benefiting from a tax exempt status under the Internal Revenue Code. Reg. § 2.12, 40 Fed. Reg. 27806 (1975).

38. TASC Legal Analysis, *supra* note 18, at Part II, pg. 29.

39. Reg. § 2.11, 40 Fed. Reg. 27804-05 (1975).

40. See, e.g., N.Y. MENTAL HYGIENE LAW § 81.19 (e) (Supp. 1974). See also the discussion of state legislation at page 105 *infra.*

41. Ex parte Copeland, 91 Tex. Crim. 549, 240 S.W. 314 (1922).

42. *See generally* MCCORMICK, EVIDENCE § 143 (1972); Annot. 13 A.L.R.2d 1439 (1950). *See also* Apodaca v. Viramontes, 53 N.M. 514, 212 P.2d 425 (1949).

43. *Id.*

44. People v. Bogolowski, 326 Ill. 253, 157 N.E. 181 (1927).

45. Santobello v. New York, 404 U.S. 257 (1971). The court here dealt with the problem of one prosecutor making a promise during plea negotiations and another prosecutor, unaware of the original promise, not complying with the original plea agreement. The court noted that the second prosecutor is bound by the original agreement. However, the hazards of building diversion programs on de facto prosecutorial immunity doctrines should be recognized.

46. See discussion at page 36, *infra*, for a consideration of the level of governmental coercion that will preclude an individual from being a true volunteer.

47. *See* N.Y. MENTAL HYGIENE LAW § 81.19 (a) (Supp. 1974): "Every person charged with a crime who, while in custody or when he appears before the court, shall state, indicate, or show symptoms or it otherwise appears, that he is a narcotic addict, shall undergo a medical examination to determine whether he is a narcotic addict. The commission shall designate facilities and establish procedures for the conduct of such medical examinations and shall provide for the use therein of accepted medical procedures, tests, and treatment, which may include but are not limited to narcotic antagonists and thin layer chromotography. Such medical examination shall take place with all reasonable speed after the person is arrested or brought before the court."

48. Medical technology may soon make it possible to force the in-

voluntary expulsion of a urine sample without the use of physical force. On the other hand, urine expulsion is a bodily necessity and thus separate issues may arise where programs collect and test urine samples of all arrestees without consent although the expulsion itself is left to nature. There are, of course, means using physical force to extract urine samples, including use of a catheter or direct extraction from the bladder by insertion of a needle through the abdominal wall.

49. 342 U.S. 165 (1952).

50. 352 U.S. 432 (1957).

51. 384 U.S. 757 (1966).

52. The issue has not as yet been directly raised in the context of an addict diversion program. A California case specifically rejected a due process attack on a urine test conducted upon a sample voluntarily given to a parole officer. People v. Saldivar, 249 Cal. App.2d 670, 57 Cal. Rptr. 731 (1967).

53. *See generally* Note, *Constitutional Limitations on the Taking of Body Evidence*, 78 YALE L.J. 1074 (1969); Annot: *Requiring Submission to Physical Examination or Test as Violation of Constitutional Rights*, 25 A.L.R. 2d 1407 (1952). *See* Blackford v. United States, 247 F.2d 745 (9th Cir. 1957) (rectal search not violative); Brent v. White, 398 F.2d 503 (5th Cir. 1968), cert. denied, 393 U.S. 1123 (1969) (blood, tissue and saliva samples not violative); Blefare v. United States, 362 F.2d 870 (9th Cir. 1966) (use of emetic not violative, but see dissent suggesting the process was savage).

Some cases have applied *Rochin* where the facts were particularly outrageous. Where a high level of physical force is used in addition to the normal testing procedure, courts have precluded use of the evidence. Huguez v. United States, 406 F.2d 366 (9th Cir. 1968) (rectal search with force.) And in Guy v. McCauley, 16 CRIM. L. RPTR. 2290 (E.D. Wisc. 1974) the court was "shocked" at testimony that a nonmedically trained policewoman routinely "searched all the privates of all female prisoners."

54. 384 U.S. 757 (1966).

55. *Id.* at 765.

56. In a slightly different context, the Supreme Court in *Schmerber* did recognize that a chemical test can be so intertwined with testimony as to either preclude the test or to preclude use of the testimony. *See id.* at 765 n. 9. *See also* State v. Andrews, 212 N.W.2d 863 (Minn. 1973) where the Minnesota Supreme Court held, notwithstanding, *Schmerber*, that the Fifth Amendment prohibits admission into evidence testimony that the defendant refused to submit to chemical testing. *Contra*, People v. Ellis, 65 Cal.2d 529, 421 P.2d 393, 55 Cal. Rptr. 385 (1966).

57. 384 U.S. 757 (1966).

58. *Id.* at 767. *See also* Cupp v. Murphy, 412 U.S. 291 (1973) (scraping of fingernails is search within Fourth Amendment).

59. TASC Legal Analysis, *supra* note 18, at Part III, pgs. 14-15. The only case the study cites for the proposition advanced is Martell v. Klingman, 11 Wis.2d 296, 105 N.W.2d 446 (1960). The study says the case held that "having a suspect urinate in a bottle under the impression that the police officers holding the bottle were merely attempting to help the suspect relieve himself would not be violative of the Fourth Amendment protections." *Id.* at 15. The case is hardly supportive of either the argument advanced or the description just quoted. The case involved the introduction of the test results in a civil case rather than a criminal case; the court dealt with the Wisconsin Constitution rather than the Fourth Amendment; and, most importantly, the case was decided long before the Fourth Amendment was even held applicable to the states through the Fourteenth. *See* Ker v. California, 374 U.S. 23 (1963).

60. TASC Legal Analysis, *supra* note 18, at Part III, pg. 14.

61. 389 U.S. 347 (1967).

62. *Id.* at 351–52.

63. *Id.* at 357. The quote has often been utilized by the Court and was recently reaffirmed. *See* Schneckloth v. Bustamonte, 412 U.S. 218 (1973).

64. Watkins v. United States, 354 U.S. 178 (1957).

65. Terry v. Ohio, 392 U.S. 1 (1968).

66. Adams v. Williams, 407 U.S. 143 (1972) (stop and superficial search revealing unlicensed weapon justified by informant's tip that the subject was armed and in possession of narcotics).

67. A case not easily categorized is Cupp v. Murphy, 412 U.S. 291 (1973). Here the officers were investigating the strangulation slaying of the defendant's wife. While questioning defendant an officer noticed a dark spot on defendant's finger, and against defendant's will, took a scraping of defendant's fingernail. While probable cause existed to arrest defendant prior to the scraping, an actual arrest was not effectuated. The Court validated the search as one designed to prevent the destruction of evanescent evidence. While citing Terry v. Ohio, the Court appeared to rely more heavily on Chimel v. California, 395 U.S. 752 (1969), and the search "incident to an arrest" cases. It is doubtful that *Cupp* can be read to authorize investigatory searches to preserve evidence in the diversion screening context.

68. 370 F. Supp. 934 (D.D.C 1974), *rev'd*, 518 F.2d 466 (D.C. Cir. 1975).

69. 370 F. Supp. at 938.

70. *Id.* at 939.

71. *Id.* at 941. *See also* United States v. Ruiz, 23 U.S.C.M.A. 181, 48 C.M.R. 797 (1974). The court there held an order directing soldiers to give urine samples as part of a drug-abuse prevention program illegal under

the ban on forced self-incrimination of Article 31 of the Code of Military Justice. The appellate court in *Callaway* found *Ruiz* inapposite because it dealt with Fifth not Fourth Amendment rights. 518 F.2d at 475–76, n.22.

72. 518 F.2d at 474, quoting Parker v. Levy, 417 U.S. 733 at 758 (1974).

73. 518 F.2d at 476–77. It has been argued that urinalysis sampling could be conducted as an adjunct to the normal processing of inmates into jail facilities as part of a physical examination and routine booking procedure. The district court in *Callaway* drew a clear distinction between the drug-inspection program and the normal Army inspection. "Such distinguishing features as the use of dogs, strip skin examinations, and detailed intrusion into a soldier's personal effects take this procedure out of the narrow exemption from traditional Fourth Amendment restrictions that has been carved out for legitimate inspections." 370 F. Supp. at 939. The legal analysis of diversion programs developed for the Special Action Office of Drug Abuse Prevention relies on the normal procedures of induction into the Army as support for the compulsory urinalysis of pretrial detainees. TASC Legal Analysis, *supra* note 18, at Part III, pg. 23.

74. Almeida-Sanchez v. United States, 413 U.S. 266 (1973). *See also* Carroll v. United States, 267 U.S. 132, 154 (1925): "Travellers may be so stopped in crossing an international boundary because of national self-protection reasonably requiring one entering the country to identify himself as entitled to come in, and his belongings as effects which may be lawfully brought in."

75. United States v. Guadalupe-Garza, 421 F.2d 876 (9th Cir. 1970) (invalidating a strip search and use of emetic where no probable cause existed to single individual out).

76. United States v. Epperson, 454 F.2d 769 (4th Cir. 1972).

77. People v. Kuhn, 33 N.Y.2d 203, 306 N.E.2d 777 (1973).

78. United States v. Robinson, 414 U.S. 218 (1973). *See also* Davis v. Mississippi, 394 U.S. 721 (1969), where the Court made clear that the arrest must be lawful in order to support a search. In *Davis* police arrested a large number of persons in a dragnet operation to obtain fingerprints. Fingerprinting under such circumstances, the Court declared, violated the Fourth Amendment. *But see*, Cupp v. Murphy, 412 U.S. 291 (1973) where a limited search without an arrest was validated.

79. Chimel v. California, 395 U.S. 752, 762–763 (1969).

80. 414 U.S. 218 (1973).

81. *Id.* at 235.

82. State v. Kaluna, 520 P.2d 51 (Haw. 1974). In *Kaluna* the defendant was arrested on suspicion of armed robbery. At the police station she was placed in the custody of a matron who conducted a search of her per-

son and effects. During the search the defendant pulled out a piece of folded tissue paper from her brassiere and handed it to the matron. The matron unfolded the paper discovering barbituates, the illegal possession of which served as the basis for a criminal prosecution. The court held the warrantless search was not justified either as a search incident to an arrest or as a preincarceration search, rejecting for purposes of state constitutional interpretation the majority view in *Robinson. See also* People v. Kelly, 77 Misc.2d 264, 353 N.Y.S.2d 111 (Crim. Ct. 1974).

83. 384 U.S. 757 (1966).

84. *Id.* at 769–70.

85. Hawkins v. Kuhne, 153 A.D. 256, 137 N.Y.S. 1090 (1912), aff'd, 208 N.Y. 555, 101 N.E. 1104 (1913).

86. It appears that even free citizens under certain circumstances can be subjected to such procedures. In two recent cases the Supreme Court has held that physical characteristics of individuals are not subject to Fourth Amendment protections. United States v. Dionisio, 410 U.S. 1 (1973) (grand jury subpoenas for voice samples); United States v. Mara, 410 U.S. 19 (1973) (grand jury subpoenas for handwriting exemplars). These decisions rely on Katz v. United States, 389 U.S. 347 (1967), which suggested that Fourth Amendment privileges do not apply to personal traits or characteristics because there is no expectation of privacy involved. It appears the Special Action Office document incorrectly interprets *Dionisio* and *Mara* as supporting judicial orders requiring the protection of such information in all contexts and that this interpretation would thus support urine sampling. TASC Legal Analysis, *supra* note 18, at Part III, pgs. 19–20. The public aspect of fingerprints, handwriting samples, and voice prints cannot so easily be construed to include urine. The person's expectation of privacy would appear to be substantial regarding excretory functions. *See also* United States v. Laub Baking Co., 283 F. Supp. 217 (N.D. Ohio 1968), holding that because postarrest fingerprinting for identification is not conducted for an "evidentiary purpose" federal marshals have inherent authority to fingerprint even those misdemeanants who are not taken into pretrial custody: "[R]easonable police procedures, performed to effectuate a governmental interest other than the discovery of incriminating evidence, do not constitute a search within the meaning of the Fourth Amendment. And they do not become a search merely because in the course of these activities, evidence is discovered." But, whether addict identification urinalysis is analyzed as a "search" or a "nonsearch," the standard of reasonableness applies. It is unlikely that procedures under which a suspect was compelled to discharge urine would be analyzed in the same terms as minimally intrusive fingerprinting techniques.

87. *See, e.g.,* United States v. Evans, 359 F.2d 776 (3d. Cir. 1966);

Rigney v. Hendrick, 355 F.2d 710 (3d. Cir. 1965); and People v. Nelson, 225 N.E.2d 820 (Ill. Ct. App. 1967). These decisions, based on the reasoning that since the jail is a place where the detainee has no justified expectation of privacy, in-jail lineups do not infringe a detainee's fourth amendment rights, appear to mark a tentative outside limit on the state's power to make routine forced "searches" of pretrial prisoners. Their rationale has been sharply criticized by Judge Freedman, dissenting in Rigney v. Hendrick, *supra*, and reasserting his earlier opinion in Butler v. Crumlish, 229 F. Supp. 665 (E.D. Pa. 1964). The view that a detainee cannot be placed in a lineup against his will in a matter other than that in connection with which he was detained, unless police or prosecution can make the same probable cause showing which would be required for an independent arrest, was also the basis of the holding in Application of Mackell, 59 Misc.2d 760, 300 N.Y.S.2d 459 (S. Ct. 1969).

88. R. Singer, *Privacy, Autonomy, and Dignity in the Prison: A Preliminary Inquiry Concerning Constitutional Aspects of the Degradation Process in Our Prisons*, 21 BUFF. L. REV. 669 (1972). *See also* NATIONAL ADVISORY COMMISSION ON CRIMINAL JUSTICE STANDARDS AND GOALS, CORRECTIONS, Std. 2.7 (1972).

89. See Jacobson v. Massachusetts, 197 U.S. 11 (1905), upholding compulsory vaccination for smallpox in the free community.

90. 415 U.S. 800 (1974).

91. *Id.* at 807–08. *See contra*, State v. Kaluna, *supra* note 82.

92. *Id.* at 810.

93. *See* Anderson v. Nosser, 438 F.2d 183 (5th Cir. 1971).

94. The Special Action Office publication advances these two interests as supporting warrantless searches. See, TASC Legal Analysis, *supra* note 18, at Part III, pg. 17, where it is proposed that an individual's right to privacy must be balanced against the safe and efficient administration of the jails, citing United States v. Krapf, 285 F.2d 647 (3d. Cir. 1961), in which a *convicted* person challenged the right of a United States Marshal to fingerprint him. See also TASC Legal Analysis, Part III, pg. 16 where Jacobson v. Massachusetts, *supra* note 89, is cited to support the jail house booking procedure. *Jacobson* validated compulsory vaccination for smallpox in the free community, but vaccination and seizure are two separate categories of activities.

See TASC Legal Analysis, Part III, pg. 22, where the argument is advanced that withdrawal can be detected by mandatory urine sampling in order to insure proper medical care for inmates and to avoid exposure of "officials and the governmental unit to liabilities for damages resulting to the arrestee and those around him." Providing the opportunity for drug treatment would avoid liability to the arrestee and is far different from compulsory treatment or testing. And as suggested in the text, there are far less intrusive means of protecting other inmates.

95. Urine sampling has been questioned as an effective means of addict identification. See *supra* note 3.

96. See page 33, *infra*.

97. 359 U.S. 360 (1959).

98. 387 U.S. 523 (1967).

99. 387 U.S. 541 (1967).

100. *Id.* at 538.

101. United States v. Biswell, 406 U.S. 311 (1972).

102. Wyman v. James, 400 U.S. 309 (1971).

103. *Supra* note 101.

104. *Id.* at 316.

105. *Id.*

106. Citing North American Cold Storage Co. v. Chicago, 211 U.S. 306 (1908).

107. Colonade Catering Corp. v. United States, 397 U.S. 72 (1970).

108. Even where the safety of a police officer is concerned, the courts have required that at least some reasonable suspicion be present before a stop and frisk of a person be conducted. Terry v. Ohio, 392 U.S. 1 (1968). See also Williams v. Alioto, 15 CRIM. L. RPTR. 2187 (N.D. Cal. 1974), where stopping of all black males matching a description of the "Zebra" killer in San Francisco was limited by Fourth Amendment standards.

109. *See, e.g.*, Dole, *Detoxification of Sick Addicts in Prison*, 220 J.A.M.A. 366 (1972); Kozel, DuPont & Brown, *Narcotics and Crime: A Study of Narcotic Involvement in an Offender Population*, 7 INT'L J. OF THE ADDICTIONS 443 (1972).

110. *See* Williams v. Alioto, *supra* note 108.

111. Committee for G.I. Rights v. Callaway, 518 F.2d 466 (D.C. Cir. 1975).

112. Hamilton v. Love, 328 F. Supp. 1182 (E.D. Ark. 1971). *See also* NATIONAL ADVISORY COMMISSION ON CRIMINAL JUSTICE STANDARDS AND GOALS, CORRECTIONS, Std. 4.9 (1972) (recommending that all pretrial programs of treatment be voluntary).

113. Williams v. Alioto, 15 CRIM. L. RPTR. 2187 (N.D. Cal. 1974). The unsolved and apparently race related "Zebra" murders did not justify a lessening of Fourth Amendment standards for stop and frisk.

114. Jacobson v. Massachusetts, 197 U.S. 11 (1905).

115. Compagnie Francaise de Navigation a Vapeur v. Louisiana State Board of Health, 186 U.S. 380 (1902).

116. Kroplin v. Truax, 119 Ohio St. 610, 165 N.E. 498 (1929).

117. North American Cold Storage Co. v. Chicago, 211 U.S. 306 (1908).

118. Criticism that this argument is raised here as a straw to be easily dealt with would be justified were it not for the citation of *Jacobson* in TASC Legal Analysis, *supra* note 18, at Part III, pg. 16.

119. Camara v. Municipal Court, 387 U.S. 523, 539 (1967).

120. TASC Legal Analysis, *supra* note 18, at Part III, pg. 24.

121. Bivens v. Six Unknown Named Agents of Federal Bureau of Narcotics, 403 U.S. 388 (1971).

122. *See, e.g.* Lankford v. Gelston, 364 F.2d 197 (4th Cir. 1966); Williams v. Alioto, 15 CRIM. L. RPTR. 2187 (N.D. Cal. 1974).

123. *See* page 9, *supra.*

124. *Id.*

125. 384 U.S. 436 (1966).

126. Indeed, the continued stability of Miranda was recently put in question in Michigan v. Tucker, 417 U.S. 433 (1974).

127. 412 U.S. 218 (1973).

128. *Id.* at 231.

129. *Id.* at 232.

130. *Id.*

131. *Id.*

132. *Id.* at 241.

133. 190 F.2d 649 (D.C. Cir. 1951).

134. *Id.* at 651. *See* United States v. Watson, 504 F.2d 849 (9th Cir. 1974), recognizing that *Schneckloth* is not applicable to custodial searches.

135. *See, e.g.,* United States v. Heimforth, 493 F.2d 970 (9th Cir. 1974); Hayes v. Cady, 500 F.2d 1212 (7th Cir. 1974). In United States v. Bolin, 514 F.2d 554 (7th Cir. 1975), the court found that a threat to arrest the accused's girl friend if consent to a search of his home was not given invalidated the search, particularly because the threat was made while the accused was in custody.

136. United States v. Smith, 395 F. Supp. 1155, 1157 (W.D.N.Y. 1975).

3

Legal Issues in Selection and Admission of Persons into Diversion Programs

Eligibility Requirements and Equal Protection

Addict-diversion programs offering deferred or adjourned prosecution during treatment are relatively selective. Whether the legal mechanism by which defendants are admitted to addict-diversion programs is judicial (as when a "diversion hearing" is held in each case and all referrals are accomplished by court order) or administrative (as when the decision to divert is at the discretion of a prosecutor or a treatment program official, or requires the concurrence of both), a variety of "eligibility criteria" are employed to sift the defendants who will be permitted to volunteer from those who will not. Among the criteria most commonly employed are the defendant's age, place of residence, past record of convictions, current charge, prior participation in treatment on conditioned bond, and "treatability" or "motivation." Depending on program design these criteria may be made express or employed as unstated guidelines by decision makers.[1]

The possibility of a challenge under the Equal Protection Clause of the Fourteenth Amendment must be considered whenever a state-sponsored program operates to discriminate among classes of persons,[2] whether by its terms or as a result of the manner in which it is implemented,[3] or in the distribution of burdens or benefits.[4] In any inquiry into the equal protection aspects of a discriminatory program or practice, the first test is whether the program is implemented to further a practice that is permissible for government to pursue. Addict-diversion programs obviously measure up to this threshold standard. Whether initiated in the legislature or by functionaries of the criminal justice system, such programs are not inherently offensive since they are not intended primarily to promote inequality or to further any unconstitutional objective; to the contrary, such programs have the legitimate public objectives of conferring special and valuable benefits on individual defendants and on the community.

Past the threshold of establishing permissible purpose, the next test ordinarily applied in equal protection analysis is whether the challenged classification is reasonably related to the accomplishment of that purpose. The standard of "reasonable relationship" is applied when the classification in question is not inherently "suspect," and when the application of that classification does not affect the exercise of "fundamental rights." If the classification involves some "suspect" class, such as race, or some "fundamental right", such as the right to vote, the government must show that a compelling state interest is advanced by the classification and that that interest cannot be advanced in any less discriminatory manner.

Courts have not as yet had the opportunity directly to consider the application of the Equal Protection Clause to pretrial addict-diversion programs. Regardless of the standard employed in such analysis—whether access to diversion is a "fundamental right" demanding a compelling state interest or requires only that classifications be reasonably related to a legitimate governmental purpose—several commonly employed eligibility criteria raise issues of potential constitutional dimension. Of course, any criteria that systematically discriminate against persons on the basis of race or religion are unconstitutional. And subtler forms of classification, which result in discrimination on the basis of race, are equally impermissible. These types of classifications, representing obvious violations of the Equal Protection Clause, will not be pursued here.[5] However, other criteria, such as excluding persons with criminal records or persons charged with certain offenses, raise more difficult questions and deserve treatment. The discussion will be divided into two parts: first, a consideration of a series of cases involving a two-felony exclusion in the Narcotic Addict Rehabilitation Act culminating in *Marshall* v. *United States*,[6] decided by the United States Supreme Court; and second, a consideration of other possible approaches in applying the Equal Protection Clause to addict-diversion programs.

Excluding Repeat Offenders—The NARA Cases

The more prevalent exclusion from eligibility for diversion programs is generally one based on the offense charged or on past criminal record. In some programs, misdemeanants are preferred over persons charged with felonies;[7] in others, persons with a history of crime are excluded either by the practice of diversion staff or as a matter of law. Any equal-protection analysis of such eligibility criteria must necessarily begin with the recent United States Supreme Court decision in *Marshall* v. *United States*.[8]

The *Marshall* decision dealt with the constitutionality of provisions of the Narcotic Addict Rehabilitation Act of 1966 (NARA),[9] which preclude persons with two or more felonies from treatment programs. Specifically involved in *Marshall* were the provisions of Title II, which involved sentencing of any defendant convicted in federal court.[10] NARA provides that the sentencing judge can sentence convicted addict-defendants to therapeutic, correctional programs. In order to do this the judge has to find that the candidate is fit for rehabilitation. However, by the terms of the statute, persons with two or more prior felony convictions are automatically ineligible for the lesser sentence to addict-rehabilitation therapy programs. The petitioner, who had previously been convicted of three felonies, was denied treatment under NARA although the sentencing judge recommended he receive treatment while incarcerated. The sole basis for ineligibility was the three former felonies. Petitioner challenged his sentence on the basis that the two felony rule was a denial of equal protection. While *Marshall* dealt with Title II of NARA, which is applicable to convicted persons, Title I of the act involving preconviction diversion contains a two-felony exclusion as well.[11]

The Court in *Marshall* in a 6–3 decision found the two-felony exclusion constitutional and not a denial of equal protection. The majority first noted that the less stringent standard of "rational relationship" was applicable as no suspect classification or fundamental right was involved. The Court thus approved the court of appeals finding that there is no "fundamental right to rehabilitation."

Chief Justice Burger, writing for the majority, found a number of premises Congress could have accepted that would justify the exclusion. Among these were:

1. A person having "greater difficulty in conforming his behavior to societal rules and laws would . . . be less likely to benefit from treatment."[12]
2. A person with a long criminal record "might also pose impediments to the successful treatment of others in the program."[13]
3. Persons with fewer past crimes "may well be younger" and Congress sought to give priority to "convicted addicts at an early stage in their lives."[14]
4. Persons with long criminal records "might be potentially disruptive elements within the sensitive environment of a drug treatment program."[15]
5. "hardened" criminals might pose a "greater potential danger to society on early release."[16]
6. Limited resources should not be exploited by persons who were viewed "as primarily anti-social and only secondarily addicts."[17]
7. Persons with long criminal records have a "lesser susceptibility to deterrence."[18]

The Court also emphasized that since drug-addict treatment is by its nature "experimental" the judgment of Congress should be afforded great weight and, that in that context, the above listed premises supported the exclusion.

Three justices dissented in an opinion by Justice Marshall who disagreed, first, that the less stringent "rationally related" tests should be employed and, second, that the exclusion of persons with two prior felonies effectuated any of the legitimate legislative purposes the majority found capable of supporting the exclusion. The basic thrust of the dissent was that this kind of automatic exclusion written into legislation cannot hope to effectuate any rational purpose in the clinically complex, professionally uncertain field of drug-abuse treatment. Only discretionary application of eligibility rules could adequately implement any objective Congress might legitimately pursue. This is reflected, in part, in Justice Marshall's statement that "[i]t makes no sense to term an addict a 'hardened criminal' simply because he has engaged in criminal activity which may have been symptomatic of his addiction."[19]

It should be recognized that the majority opinion in *Marshall* does not specifically govern either Title I of NARA, which contains authorization for preconviction diversion to treatment, nor does it directly govern pretrial addict-diversion programs conducted under authority of state law. However, the case is strong evidence that at least the six majority members would regard prior criminal record exclusions as justifiable in drug-diversion programs. In fact, in the course of the opinion Chief Justice Burger cites legislative history directed at Title I as supporting his validation of Title II with the note that "the House Report indicates that there is no difference between the rationale of the language of the various provisions."[20]

It remains arguable, on the other hand, that equal protection aspects of entry barriers in preconviction diversion programs deserve even closer examination than that required in *Marshall*. While a NARA II-variety therapeutic disposition is made after conviction, at a phase of the criminal process where legislative and judicial discretion traditionally have been given wide scope,[21] diversion to treatment is definitionally a preconviction procedure in which the presumption of innocence should require the same standard of classification demanded of programs that are directed at persons outside the criminal justice system entirely. Furthermore, diversion prior to conviction is, in addition to a means of securing treatment, a separate "track" within the criminal justice process by which a person can seek disposition of criminal charges.[22] Where classifications giving preference to selected unconvicted criminal defendants are called into question, it is to be expected that they will be examined closely for reasonableness.[23] Thus, *Marshall* does not necessarily foreclose the outcome of challenges to felony exclusions in pretrial diversion programs.

The Title II cases in the courts of appeal prior to *Marshall* give helpful illustration of the difficulty courts have had with past criminal-record exclusions. A short review of these opinions serves to highlight the arguments that could be offered in the event a challenge is made to pretrial diversion exclusionary criteria.

Until the decision in *Marshall*, the constitutional status of the two-felony exclusion had been a matter of considerable confusion, much of it stemming from varying interpretations of the leading case of *Watson* v. *United States* decided by the United States Court of Appeals for the District of Columbia.[24] Before *Watson* the constitutionality of the two-felony rule had gone unchallenged.[25] *Watson* clearly turned on a finding that the two-felony exclusion of Title II, as applied to the applicant, violated Fifth Amendment guarantees of equal protection, but the application of this principle to other fact situations remained obscure. *Watson* was variously read as voiding the two-felony rule altogether;[26] as prohibiting application of the rule insofar as the prior felonies were drug-law offenses;[27] and ultimately, in *United States* v. *Hamilton*,[28] as barring application of the rule only where a disqualifying prior felony conviction predated the enactment of NARA in 1966.[29]

Subsequent to *Hamilton* the United States Court of Appeals for the Ninth Circuit, in the case of *Marshall* v. *Parker*,[30] rejected *Watson* outright, holding instead that there is no "fundamental right" to rehabilitation, and that the exclusion of two-time felons from NARA sentencing is a reasonable classification based on the justifiable legislative presumption that they are, as a class, generally less likely to respond to rehabilitative treatment. In the case of *United States* v. *Bishop*,[31] the Court of Appeals for the First Circuit held the reverse, after an analysis that relied only in part on *Watson* and its direct progeny. In *Bishop* the court concluded that a "whole series of anomalies, in the root sense of inequalities," renders the "grossly over- and underinclusive" two-felony disqualification unreasonable, as lacking in relevance to its asserted purpose as a classification. Moreover, it held squarely that the two-felony rule violated equal protection considerations whether or not the disqualifying convictions were for drug-law and drug-related offenses. The decisions in *Marshall* and *Bishop* represented two diametrically opposed judicial positions on the constitutionality of prior-record eligibility criteria in addiction-treatment schemes that recruit from the criminal justice system.[32]

In its decision in *Marshall* v. *Parker*, the Ninth Circuit Court of Appeals chose to defer to what it found might have been a rational congressional purpose in laying down the two-felony rule:

Standards of eligibility may well have been developed by the experts in the field with an eye toward restricting elgibility in the beginning to those most likely to be rehabilitated and who would appear to bring to the program the greater promise for its success, consistent with time, money, trained personnel and facilities which the Congress believed were available for it. For these reasons (or others) the Congress might well have established a policy to exclude, at least at the start, those whose known criminal careers make them undue risks for rehabilitation, and undue risks for the success of the program and to others in it.

Opinions might differ as to where the line should be drawn. Some might raise the limits of eligibility by admitting those with a record of only one prior conviction for a crime of violence and raising the exclusion based on prior felonies from two to five and eliminating prior narcotics counts from the standard. Congress chose, for reasons we cannot determine to be arbitrary, to establish the lines of eligibility where we now find them. Here the Congress is not depriving citizens of rights which they have always held and rights which are fundamental to them as members of our society. The court in *Watson* would simply extend the program farther. So might we, were we acting in a legislative capacity.[33]

In *Bishop* the First Circuit Court of Appeals also denied that the NARA two-felony rule affected fundamental rights or involved suspect classification. Like the Ninth Circuit, it looked to the reasonableness of the rule in light of the purpose of NARA. But its inquiry examined more closely the relevant legislative history in its medical and legal contexts. Noting that the apparent aim of Congress in establishing eligibility criteria was to "[a]ssist the courts in making distinctions between hardened addict–criminals deserving punishment, and other addict–criminals deserving consideration for treatment," the court proceeded to observe that the Congress had taken cognizance of the fact that "narcotics addiction almost inevitably compels its victims to turn to crime and is a factor in practically all crime that addicts commit."[34] In the light of this inevitable connection between addiction and crime, the court found the blanket two-felony exclusion irrelevant to the congressional purpose. In particular it observed the rule is one which admits a person who

sells heroin for his own addiction . . . even though he had once previously, while not yet addicted, conspired to transport forged checks in interstate commerce as part of an illegal business, while [barring] one who had twice so previously conspired solely to get the funds necessary to support his addiction,[35]

which operates "to include a one-time violent offender but excludes a two-time non-violent offender,"[36] and which, by its incorporation of the varying statutory definitions of "felony" crimes employed in state criminal codes, implies the result that "two persons who both twice previously committed the identical crime of possession of marijuana might be treated differently."[37] Further, the court noted critically the "disregard for all time limits" of the two-felony rule as "further evidence of the classification's irrationality:"

All prior felonies are counted—whether a joyride by a peer imitating teenager or a rape committed by a 35-year-old sex deviant during the pendency of the proceedings in which sentence is about to be imposed. Any intervening period of good behavior or attempts at rehabilitation are ignored.[38]

In sum, the First Circuit did not rule that all eligibility criteria, or even all criteria related to an analysis of an addict's criminal history, are per se unconstitutional. It did hold that a valid exclusionary device must not be so crudely designed that it inevitably passes large numbers of the very "hardened criminals" it is designed to screen out, while blocking the way to "treatable addicts" who are the chance victims of fixed mathematical formulae.

In its consideration of *Marshall*, the Supreme Court divided along the lines already indicated by the courts of appeals. The holding in *Marshall* was limited to NARA's Title II, which deals exclusively with postconviction therapeutic sentencing. The balancing of the opinion of the Court as to the validity of the two-felony rule as applied to NARA's diversionary Title I cannot be gauged from the opinions in *Marshall*. Even more difficult to assess is how the Court would divide on an equal protection challenge to a felony-record exclusion employed in a local addict-diversion program.

In such a challenge several of the significant factors in *Marshall* might be absent. Unlike the NARA two-felony rule, the exclusionary criteria of local addict-diversion programs may be administrative rather than legislative in origin. In other equal protection challenges to nonlegislative classifications, the courts have employed a test that looks to the classifiers' real intentions and expectations,[39] rather than searching out a hypothetical but justifiable purpose. Thus, the Court might hold diversion administrators to a standard of rational justification significantly higher than that to which it held the Congress in *Marshall*.

Not every diversionary program will be well situated to justify draconian exclusionary criteria by reference to the need to allocate scarce treatment resources. NARA II treatment now is limited to approximately 600 beds in federal correctional institutions;[40] by contrast, local addict-diversion programs linked with facilities for outpatient treatment may have no fixed ceiling on referral capacity.

The majority opinion in *Marshall* is unsatisfactory in a number of respects, but it does serve at present to support the validity of past criminal record exclusions.[41] However, it is important to note that none of the premises cited by the chief justice as supportive of the rationality of the exclusion are buttressed by any facts to show that they are accurate. No evidence is cited that persons with two prior felonies are more disruptive, less treatable, less deterrable, or less amenable to the processes of addict diversion. The force of the dissent that broad mandatory exclusions inevitably lead to counterproductive results cannot be diminished by unsupported assertions to the contrary. However, as long as a majority of the Court is willing to stand by the decision, future challenges to prior felony exclusions may need to be based on factual proof that the premises asserted for the exclusion are inaccurate.

Other Considerations—A New Track in the Criminal Process

The *Marshall* case clearly indicates that a person has no "fundamental right" to rehabilitation, which would call forth the more stringent standard of equal protection analysis. Again, however, *Marshall* dealt with the sentencing of a person already convicted of a criminal offense. No court has yet considered whether programs that divert persons prior to trial or conviction involve additional considerations, which may require more compelling evidence to justify exclusionary criteria.

Were addict diversion a medical or social rehabilitation service only, the *Marshall* decision would provide a forceful answer. Addict diversion, however, along with providing a practical mechanism for delivering rehabilitative care, creates what may be termed a "new track" within the criminal process, running parallel to the conventional track, which leads from charge, through plea or trial, to sentencing. Although diversion often is popularly termed an "alternative" *to* criminal processing, addict diversion at least is more properly considered as an alternative *in* criminal processing. After an addict is diverted to treatment, he remains subject to court jurisdiction and potential prosecution; whereas a defendant subject to conventional prosecution gains a favorable disposition through asserting a defense or engaging in negotiations, the divertee earns a favorable disposition by demonstrating to the court his progress toward personal rehabilitation. Novel as this innovation may be, it is an innovation intimately tied to the courts and the traditional institutions of criminal justice.

At stake during the "intake phase" of any addict-diversion program is something more than the accused's interest in preferential rehabilitative treatment. Also involved is his interest in being permitted to submit himself to a particular procedure for the disposition of criminal cases on terms of substantial equality with other alleged offenders. If this interest, which may be termed an interest in equal "access to the criminal justice system," is deemed to be "fundamental," constitutionally permissable discriminatory restrictions on its exercise must be more than "reasonable." They must meet the stricter test of "compelling" necessity.

The Supreme Court has not determined in what circumstances—if any—access to established institutions and procedures of the criminal justice system is to be considered a fundamental interest for the purposes of equal protection analysis. While it might seem obvious, for example, that a state's legislative denial of jury trials to certain felony offenders would be an action repugnant to the equal protection clause of the Fourteenth Amendment, as well as to the due process clause under which state jury right cases have been resolved,[42] the Court has not had occasion to so hold. And, in the recent case of *Johnson* v. *Louisiana*,[43] the Court has intimated that where access to state jury trial is granted on different terms to different offenders, the equal protection standard by which these differentials are to be assessed is one less exacting than the strict scrutiny test traditionally applied in the sphere of fundamental interests.[44]

Nevertheless, although access to the process of criminal courts is not yet a fundamental interest recognized as an equivalent to the right of interstate travel or the right to vote, there also are indications that it has been afforded special status as an "important" interest, different in kind from the various personal and commercial interests traditionally viewed as nonfundamental. These indications come in the line of Supreme Court cases beginning with *Griffin* v. *Illinois*,[45] which held that a state's refusal to provide transcripts of criminal trials to indigent appellants denied them equal protection by barring their access to full direct appellate review. The decisions that followed, all variations on the theme of *Griffin*, struck down a variety of procedural barriers to appellate review raised by the states against indigents.[46]

The peculiar importance of these decisions to a consideration of diversion is that they deal with state appellate review, a "track" within the criminal process that, although traditional, is not constitutionally mandated in itself. The Court has summed up this aspect of their cumulative significance in *Rinaldi* v. *Yeager*:

This Court has never held that the States are required to establish avenues of appellate review, but it is now fundamental that, once established, these avenues must be kept free of unreasoned distinctions that can only impede open and free access to the courts.[47]

If this is true of access to the courts during the postconviction phase of criminal proceedings, it is at least arguably the rule governing diversion as well. No community is compelled to divert addicts from the criminal justice system; having chosen to do so, however, it may be under a special obligation to clear this new track of unjustifiable barriers.

The other present significance of the Court's decisions concerning appellate review is that in them the "strict scrutiny" standard of equal protection analysis, usually reserved for cases involving fundamental interests or suspect classifications, has been employed. Although it has been suggested that this use of the strict standard is explained by the fact that these decisons involved special limitations imposed on indigents, and thus involved a suspect classification, this explanation is incomplete. As Justice Marshall recently wrote, dissenting in the case of *San Antonio Independent School District* v. *Rodriquez*, where a majority of the Court had undertaken to reexamine and restrict its doctrine of "fundamental interests":

[D]iscrimination adversely affecting access to appellate process which a State has chosen to provide has been considered to require close judicial scrutiny. See, e.g., *Griffin* v. *Illinois, supra*; *Douglas* v. *California*, 372, U.S. 353 (1963).

It is true that *Griffin* and *Douglas* also involved discrimination against indigents, that is, wealth discrimination. But as the majority points out, the Court has never deemed wealth discrimination alone to be sufficient to require strict judicial scrutiny; rather, such review of wealth classifications has been applied only when the discrimination affects an important individual interest, see, *e.g.*, *Harper* v. *Virginia Bd. of Elections*, 383 U.S. 663 (1966). Thus, I believe *Griffin* and *Douglas* can only be understood as premised on a recognition of the fundamental importance of the criminal appellate process.[48]

The implications of the appellate review cases for the future of equal protection litigation involving access to the criminal process are difficult to gauge. It is unlikely that these cases now will be given such a broad reading that, by analogy, the organizers of diversion programs will be required to justify every eligibility criterion imposed as fulfilling a compelling state interest. Indeed, the decision in *Rodriquez*, which offers an equation of "fundamental right[s]" to specific "rights and liberties protected by the Constitution,"[49] may be read as foreclosing for the moment any judicial movement toward the view that access to special tracks within the criminal justice system is a fundamental right. Alternatively, it may develop that restrictions affecting important but arguably nonfundamental interests will be subjected to close scrutiny, but only where they also involve a suspect classification or one such as wealth, which is less than "suspect" but more than benign.[50] Finally, it is possible that the courts will avoid the analytic dichotomy between strict scrutiny and permissive review in some equal protection cases, embracing instead a "balancing" test, which demands justifications that are less than compelling but more than merely reasonable when the interests at stake are important but not fundamental.[51]

Whatever the future direction of equal protection analysis in the area of access to the courts, all eligibility criteria will remain open to challenge on the ground of arbitrariness, and the criteria discussed at length above—particularly prior-record restrictions—will remain particularly vulnerable. In addition, other administratively serviceable restrictions that are not strictly necessary to the administration of an addict-diversion program may be challenged as overly restrictive in their impact on individual access to the courts. Designers and administrators of local programs should be prepared to justify eligibility criteria involving offenders' ages, prior treatment records, social or work histories, and other personal characteristics on bases more substantial than cost-benefit projections.

Drug Treatment as a Condition of Pretrial Release

Release to a pretrial-diversion program may occur after or apart from bail proceedings. In addition, however, entry into a drug-treatment program may be a condition of release on bail. Refusal to enter a treatment program would mean detention while awaiting trial and might also preclude consideration for diversion to a drug-treatment program with subsequent dismissal of the prosecution.[52] Three distinct practical ends are served by requiring identified drug users to submit to treatment as a condition of pretrial release in addition to or in lieu of complying with other court-imposed financial or nonfinancial conditions. First, the practice is intended to reduce the incidence of drug-related offenses committed by defendants awaiting disposition on other charges. Second, it aims to introduce a large number of drug abusers identified during criminal process to the benefits of treatment, at least for the limited period between arraignment and disposition. Third, it enables the staff of addict-diversion programs to identify those addict–defendants whose postarraignment treatment records indicate that they are likely candidates for participation in continuing therapy on a deferred or adjourned prosecution basis.[53]

The promotion of a general policy favoring pretrial release is cited as an additional, second-order justification for the use of the treatment-conditioned bond. It is suspected that in some jurisdictions defendants known informally to a bail-setting officer as drug abusers are denied pretrial release as a matter of unstated policy; the device most commonly employed is the requirement of a secured cash bond in a high amount.[54] It has been suggested that if there exist treatment-conditioned bond programs, more of these defendants can be released on personal recognizance bonds, on unsecured cash bonds, or on secured cash bonds in reasonable amounts. Worthy as such practical objectives are, however, their accomplishment through the use of the treatment-conditioned bond nevertheless threatens to infringe certain protected rights of persons accused of crimes: (1) the right to bail in noncapital cases; (2) the right to be free of demands for excessive bail; and (3) the right of the unconvicted to reject state interference in the form of treatment. Analysis of these issues must center at the outset on the permissible function of pretrial bail.

The scope of the right to bail depends on the application of state constitutional and statutory provisions as well as the Eighth Amendment provision, which provides that "Excessive bail shall not be required. . . ." It is not proposed to review or to add to the legal literature directed at the existence or the extent of a "right to bail".[55] The implications of the various viewpoints on this subject for addict-diversion programs generally, and drug-related conditions particularly, will be considered.

Whether the admission to pretrial bail is deemed a matter of right[56] or a matter of discretion,[57] a requirement of "excessive bail" is impermissible everywhere.[58] The prohibition against "excessive bail" is violated not only by the fixing of conditions more stringent than are required to fulfill the purpose of bail; it is also violated by a determination of conditions of release based on factors which are irrelevant to the accomplishment of that purpose.[59]

The view that for many years has prevailed regarding the legal application of the right to bail is that persons are entitled to release on bail and that the sole function of bail is to insure the presence of the defendant at his trial. Under this view, conditions unrelated to this purpose would be void. The other view, expressed in the literature and some recent legislation, is that release pending trial can be conditioned on a number of factors in addition to insuring the return of the defendant.[60] Most prominent among the additional factors urged as constitutional is the "dangerousness" of the defendant. Of course, if bail can serve a wide variety of purposes, then conditions relating to drug treatment are more easily defended. If the only function of bail is to insure the defendant's presence at trial, then any drug-treatment condition must be based on that function and on that function only. The United States Supreme Court has not spoken authoritatively on the scope of the right to bail, and thus the procedures of diversion programs can only be analyzed tentatively.[61]

In most state jurisdictions the only recognized function of bail is to insure the presence of the defendant at trial.[62] Under this view it is generally impermissable to impose special burdens on a drug-dependent defendant merely to discourage his commission of drug-related crimes while awaiting trial, to introduce him to the benefits of treatment, or to facilitate administration of a diversion plan. Special drug-related conditions could only be justified if they in fact related to the likelihood of his appearance in court.

As a broad generalization, it can be stated that there is no empirical evidence to justify an invariable judicial assumption that a defendant's drug dependence increases the likelihood that the defendant will fail to appear for trial. As a matter of speculation, it can be argued that because a drug-dependent individual (or more specifically, a heroin addict) is particularly likely to engage in criminal activity to support his habit in the period between arraignment and trial, he will be more likely than the non-addicted defendant to have acquired special cause to avoid surrendering himself to the authorities on the trial date.[63] It can be asserted to the same effect that a history of drug use is frequently indicative of personal instability or irresponsibility. However, it can be argued that addicted defendants in general may be particularly good risks for pretrial release because their ties to the local drug distribution system and their need for a continuing drug supply make flight from their home jurisdiction an unattractive prospect. Thus, it cannot be said that drug addiction is so clearly relevant to appearance at trial that its detection makes the imposition of a special drug-related pretrial release condition appropriate in all cases. Only the individualized consideration of all cases is capable of sorting out those in which evidence of drug dependence is relevant to the issue of possible flight.

In jurisdictions where there is express statutory authorization for a consideration of an offender's "dangerousness" in the pretrial-release decision,[64] the constitutional requirement that factors given weight be relevant to the purpose of bail would seem to present no barrier to giving evidence of drug dependence (at least in the form of narcotic addiction) some consideration in every case where it appears.[65] The documented correlation between narcotics addiction and repetitive criminality is too strong and too consistent to be effectively denied as a general proposition,[66] although any individual defendant should be permitted to offer evidence demonstrating that the general proposition is inapplicable to his particular case.

Even if the threshold test of relevance were met in the case of some addict-defendants, and the fact of drug dependence thus were properly afforded weight at their pretrial-release hearings, an additional constitutional barrier would stand in the way of a uniform policy of imposing special drug-related release conditions in all such cases. A continuum of increasingly restrictive devices is available to courts seeking assurance that the purpose of bail will be fulfilled.[67] They range from release on personal recognizance to outright denial of bail (or, where an offense is bailable of right, to the setting of cash or surety bail). Constitutional prohibitions against excessive bail would appear to dictate that the officer setting terms of release employ the least restrictive device which reasonably assures that the purpose will be satisfied.[68]

Release on nonmonetary conditions falls between release on recognizance and denial of bail in restrictiveness. Moreover, some particular nonmonetary conditions, such as a requirement of submission to periodic testing for narcotics addiction, clearly impose a significantly greater burden on the releasee than do others, such as a requirement of periodic reporting to a probation department or bail agency. The federal courts, interpreting the Bail Reform Act of 1966,[69] have adopted a similar policy. In *United States* v. *Cramer*,[70] for example, the United States Court of Appeals for the Fifth Circuit held that where a defendant's character and record clearly indicated that he was an eligible candidate for personal recognizance release, the trial court was without authority to impose additional nonmonetary conditions.[71]

Although *Cramer* is not founded explicitly on constitutional prohibitions against bail, those prohibitions are nevertheless implicated in any argument rejecting one condition of pretrial release because another less restrictive or less onerous condition will adequately serve the limited purposes of bail. Most judicial interpretations of "excessive bail" clauses of the federal and state constitutions have been limited to the consideration of amounts fixed as money bail.[72] But the national tendency toward "bail reform" emphasizing the use of personal recognizance and conditions necessitates that denials of release on recognizance and impositions of particular conditions be tested against the "excessive bail" standard.

The unconvicted defendant's secured rights include a right to conduct himself as nearly as possible as though he were not the focus of a criminal prosecution.[73] For the purpose of assessing its excessiveness, the term "bail" must be defined broadly enough to embrace both monetary and nonmonetary conditions of release.[74]

Whether the purpose of bail is only to insure appearance at trial or, in addition, to insure the community against criminal conduct by an accused, it may well be satisfied for individual addict–defendants by the imposition of requirements significantly less onerous than a special drug-related condition.[75] In a given case, for example, it may be sufficient to order the defendant to report by telephone or in person to a designated private or court-affiliated custodian, to order him to keep certain hours, or to order him to restrict his movements to a delimited district. Although the fact of drug dependence initially may be relevant to the consideration of appropriate conditions of release, the availability of control and supervision techniques not specifically related to drug use may be enough to make further consideration of drug dependence irrelevant to the purpose or purposes of bail.[76]

The preceding discussion is not intended to suggest that a specialized drug-related condition will always be inappropriate; in particular cases, it may be the least restrictive appropriate condition.[77] Imposing a special drug-related condition in individual cases of necessity is clearly appropriate and constitutionally sound.

Thus, while imposition of drug-related conditions can be defended in individual cases, a uniform judicial policy of imposing drug-related release conditions on all identified drug-dependant arrestees may be open to constitutional challenge.[78] And it is the policy of uniform imposition of such conditions wherever evidence of addiction appears on the court record, which, although best designed to serve therapeutic goals efficiently in addict diversion, is also most vulnerable to attack.

Accepting the view that constitutionally acceptable procedures are available by which special drug-related conditions may be imposed individually on individual pretrial releasees, substantial questions remain as to what an addict–defendant can be required to do or undergo in order to secure his release while awaiting trial. The first thrust of any drug-related condition will be a direction to the defendant to abstain from the use of prohibited substances. In order to implement this command, and to provide for monitoring of compliance, a drug-related condition generally will also contain one of three specific additional instructions: it may order a releasee to participate in a designated addiction-therapy program; it may order him to report to a public health agency and to participate in whatever form of therapy or supervision that agency determines to be appropriate; or it may order him merely to submit to periodic urinalysis testing. In assessing the appropriateness and constitutionality of each of these alternative conditions, it is necessary to weigh the rights they tend to infringe against the state interest they serve to promote.

The state's legitimate interest in circumscribing the liberty of persons accused of crimes is limited to insuring those persons' appearance at trial and, in a few jurisdictions, insuring against dangerous conduct on their part during the pretrial period. Having determined that to secure such assurances it is necessary to regulate a particular defendant's use of narcotics during the pretrial period, a judicial officer devising a release condition cannot constitutionally proceed immediately to invoke devices that are designed primarily to accomplish the distinct goals of "cure," "rehabilitation," or "behavior change."[79] Conditions related to these state interests would run contrary to both the excessive bail provisions of the Eighth Amendment and the Due Process or Equal Protection Clauses of the Fourteenth.[80] To condition the release of a drug-dependent defendant on more restrictive terms would be additionally offensive as an attempt to exact a waiver of a fundamental constitutional right as the "price" of pretrial freedom.[81] In fact, there is some doubt as to whether the judicial officer setting terms of release may go as far as to require a drug-dependent defendant to report for periodic urinalysis.[82] This is not to say that a full range of treatment services cannot or should not be offered to such defendants during the pretrial period on a voluntary basis. If representatives of treatment programs are made available on a regular basis, it can be expected that significant numbers of these defendants will in fact volunteer, although the express conditions of their pretrial release do not require it. It is wholly appropriate for the judicial officer, once he has established a limited drug-related condition, to call the range of available voluntary treatment programs to a defendant's attention.

In exceptional cases, where the defendant's record at first appearance closely suggests a history of inability to abstain from illicit drug use under supervision, the judicial officer may be justified in concluding that only immediate short-term treatment intervention is reasonably calculated to result in pretrial abstinence and may proceed to set conditions of release accordingly. Even in these exceptional cases, the rule of the "least restrictive alternative," considered together with the uncertain prognosis of the various forms of addiction treatment, dictates that a defendant be given an opportunity to choose from among the available therapeutic regimens. No court, and indeed no physician, can say with perfect certainty that an individual will respond more favorably to methadone maintenance than to drug-free treatment in a residential therapeutic community, and only the individual can say whether he regards the regular ingestion of medication or the limitation of his freedom of movement as the greater "restriction" on his privacy and liberty. Whether the defendant's selection of a treatment modality in these exceptional cases is made in open court or after referral by the arraigning officer to a "multimodality" drug-treatment program, it is essential that the defendant be enabled to make an informed choice of treatment.[83]

Guilty Plea as a Condition For Diversion

In many diversion projects a person is required to plead guilty prior to his admission into the program.[84] An admission of guilt may be considered important for the following reasons: (1) it demonstrates a step toward "rehabilitation" through admission and presumably repentence; (2) it obviates the risk in a subsequent delayed prosecution of having witnesses unavailable or memories dimmed; (3) it lends support for the exercise of governmental power over the divertee since prior to the plea the presumption of innocence might make some aspects of supervision constitutionally suspect; and (4) it may increase the leverage of the treatment staff and prosecutor in forcing persons to remain in diversion programs.[85]

In pleading guilty a person gives up several constitutional rights including his right to a trial by jury, his right to confront witnesses against him, his right to force the state to prove his guilt beyond a reasonable doubt, and the right to remain silent and not incriminate himself.[86] All of these rights are fundamental to due process. It is clear, on the other hand, that individuals may waive their constitutional rights if such waiver is intentional, voluntary and intelligent and not one induced by threat, coercion, improper inducement, or an unauthorized promise of immunity. The legal issue involved is whether conditioning admission to a treatment program on a plea of guilty is a sufficient inducement to make the plea less than fully voluntary in a legal sense. Factually, of course, pleas in this context are not completely voluntary and may not be true admissions of guilt. The potential for dismissal of charges and immunity from further prosecution is a substantial inducement even for a person who claims his innocence of the charge for which he was arrested. Indeed, obtaining treatment for his drug addiction may be paramount to any consequences that might flow from the criminal charges. The United States Supreme Court has had great difficulty implementing the voluntary and intelligent waiver concepts in the context of a criminal justice system that relies so heavily on the plea bargain. It would seem a permissible inference that a substantial number of defendants who now plead guilty would not do so without the promise or hope of *some* benefit. The history of decisions involving government induced guilty pleas is not a consistent one, and while more recent cases seem to suggest that a guilty plea as a prerequisite to entry into a diversion program is constitutionally permissible, the question is not free from doubt.

The high water mark in the Court's sensitivity to the unhappy choices required of many criminal defendants with regard to guilty pleas is *United States* v. *Jackson*.[87] In *Jackson* the federal kidnapping statute allowed the imposition of a death penalty only if recommended by a jury. The judge could impose only a life sentence. The impact, of course, was that defendants could escape the death sentence by giving up their right to a jury trial. The Court held the death sentence provision of the statute unconstitutional as imposing an unreasonable burden on the right to a jury trial. After *Jackson*, it appeared that use of varying sentences to induce waivers of constitutional rights was impermissible.

Jackson, however, was emasculated two years later in *Brady* v. *United States*.[88] The Supreme Court held that a plea of guilty entered by a defendant charged under the same kidnapping statute involved in *Jackson* was voluntary even though the plea was entered as a device to avoid any possibility of an imposition of the death penalty.[89] The Court concluded that *Jackson* did not impose a new standard in evaluating the voluntariness of guilty pleas. This decision was affirmed in *North Carolina* v. *Alford*[90] where a plea to second-degree murder was found to be voluntary and not improperly induced, notwithstanding the defendant's protestation of innocence:

The standard [in judging whether a plea is entered voluntarily] was and remains whether the plea represents a voluntary and intelligent choice among the alternative courses of action open to the defendant.
That he would not have pleaded except for the opportunity to limit the possible penalty does not necessarily demonstrate that the plea of guilty was not the product of a free and rational choice, especially where the defendant was represented by competent counsel whose advice was that the plea would be to the defendant's advantage.[91]

Brady and *North Carolina* v. *Alford* seem to support the view that the requirement of a guilty plea as a condition precedent to diversion is valid. However, certain procedural safeguards would be required in any event. The court must be convinced that the plea represents a voluntary and intelligent choice among the alternative courses of action and that the factual circumstances surrounding the plea confirms its voluntariness.[92] The presence of an attorney to advise the accused would be a critical consideration.[93]

There are, on the other hand, a number of features of both *Brady* and *Alford* that suggest they do not foreclose the possibility that a guilty plea requirement in the context of a diversion program is unacceptable. Diversion programs do not advance the same state interests found sufficient to support the institution of plea bargaining. Similarly, the guilty plea in diversion does not serve the same function as in the normal plea bargaining leading directly to sentencing.

In *Brady* the Court notes that the advantages to the state in pleas of guilty are (1) the prompt imposition of punishment, which "after an admission of guilt may more effectively attain the objectives of punishment"; and (2) the savings of resources, which can then be conserved for cases where there are substantial issues of guilt.[94] Neither interest is present in the diversion context. Since many offenders subject to diversion will not be arrested or charged with drug-related offenses, it can hardly be asserted as a general proposition that drug treatment is a "punishment" for the offense charged. In fact, the programs of diversion are recognition of and treatment for a circumstance which in and of itself, that is, addiction, cannot be punished as criminal. To argue that a plea of guilty to larceny will make treatment for drug addiction more effective seems highly speculative. While it is true that the plea does insure promptness of treatment, in the diversion context this is so only because the diversion staff makes the plea a prerequisite. In other words, the plea of guilty is *not necessary* to avoid delay in drug treatment programs.

It is also doubtful that the plea of guilty in the diversion context results in any substantial savings in judicial resources. In fact, diversion may increase the demands on the system as a whole although certainly trial costs will be saved for those that succeed. Further, the necessities of supervision, the process of determining the success of treatment, and the multitude of other decisions periodically required in diversion programs may burden judicial resources.

The majority in *Brady* noted that it would have "serious doubts about this case if the encouragement of guilty pleas by offers of leniency substantially increased the likelihood that defendants advised by competent counsel, would falsely condemn themselves."[95] In the diversion context a guilty plea requirement may well provide an incentive for false pleas of guilty. In *Brady* the alternatives were death or life imprisonment. While it is an uneasy choice, even where the defendant is innocent but circumstantial evidence provides the possibility that a jury might convict, the choice is quite different in diversion. The defendants faced with the choice are addicts; the treatment available is directed toward their addiction. While the treatment may be unpleasant, even undesired, it is essentially treatment, while punishment is minimized. Pretrial treatment will generally—and naturally—be preferred by defendants. The choice then is not between varying degrees of punishment but more between punishment or the possibility of no punishment. Since the disparity of the choice is so great and the detriment of one alternative so minor, the incentive for inducing false pleas of guilty may be viewed as powerful, rising arguably to an unacceptable level.

It is, of course, true that the *Alford* decision expressly approved a guilty plea even in the face of a record in which the defendant continued to claim his innocence. However, the Court was careful to condition its opinion on the fact that the record also disclosed substantial evidence of guilt. In the diversion context, the thrust of the inquiry prior to the guilty plea may be more toward addiction than proving the underlying offense for which the defendant was arrested. There may be cases where strong evidence of guilt is available but this would have to be determined on a case by case basis.

There may also be a question of whether the waiver of the right to a trial can be "intelligently" made even if the court determines that the choice of diversion or prosecution does not deprive the decision of its voluntariness. In plea bargaining the plea is given in return for concessions that are relatively concrete. The defendant knows precisely what he is bargaining for and can, with the assistance of counsel, predict with reasonable accuracy the eventual outcome of his case. It is technically true that the prosecutor cannot through his promises bind the sentencing judge, but the possible decisions are relatively clearly set out. In diversion, the bargained for consideration is far less tangible and much more complex. Depending on the regulations of a particular program, the prosecutor or court may agree to do something only if the defendant "succeeds" at treatment. The definition of success in addict-diversion programs differs in importance. In some programs success in treatment may only result in the judge or prosecutor reviewing the case in light of the success without any commitments of leniency.

The proposition that a compelling state interest is advanced by a guilty plea in preserving effective prosecution (i.e., obviating the risk of unavailable witnesses or testimony dulled by the passage of time if prosecution has to be resumed) is of arguable validity. Prosecutors have long been faced with this risk as witnessed by prevailing court backlogs. Given the limited duration of most diversion programs, the argument that prosecution will be adversely affected without a plea is subject to question as a justification for the forced waiver of the paramount Fifth Amendment privilege against self-incrimination.

In the last analysis a definite conclusion on the validity of guilty pleas as a condition of diversion cannot be stated. While the plea-bargaining cases suggest they are legally permissible, a case can be made for their abolition. As a matter of policy, project planners sould carefully consider the necessity of such pleas before making then an integral and required part of the diversion program.

The Right to a Speedy Trial

The right to a speedy trial is guaranteed by the Sixth Amendment and is applicable to the states through the Fourteenth Amendment.[96] In addition to the federal constitutional provisions, the constitutions of most states expressly guarantee this right or have provisions that can be interpreted to provide such a guarantee. Generally, these are more precise than the Sixth Amendment guarantee and apply with equal strength to a defendant accused of a crime in a particular state. The Supreme Court has indicated that the right to a speedy trial vests upon arrest or formal indictment.[97] Thus, diversion programs that delay the formal proceedings during the pendency of treatment raise speedy trial issues.

In *Barker* v. *Wingo*[98] the Court considered the problems of definition of both the delay sufficient to infringe the right to a speedy trial and the factors necessary to demonstrate that the accused had waived his right. The Court rejected an inflexible time limit for purposes of the Sixth Amendment in favor of an ad hoc balancing test in which the conduct of the prosecution and the defendant is weighed, assessing such factors as length and reason for the delay, the defendant's assertion of the right, and the prejudice to him. The Court in addition recognized three interests of the defendant protected by the speedy-trial provision: (1) protection against oppressive pretrial confinement; (2) limitation on anxiety and concern of the accused; and (3) protection against the possibility that the defense will be impaired by delay. Regarding waiver of the right to speedy trial, the Court rejected an earlier line of cases, which suggested that a defendant waived his right to a speedy trial unless he made a demand on the government for acceleration of proceedings. However, the Court did note that the absence of a demand for trial by the defendant would be a relevant factor in the balancing process.

Given the length of the term of most pretrial-intervention programs, a defendant would be required to waive his right to a speedy trial in order to participate. A defendant's consent to participation in a diversion program would in all likelihood be considered an effective waiver, as long as his consent was voluntarily and intentionally given.

The interests protected by speedy trial remain in jeopardy in the diversion context. Oppressive pretrial incarceration is replaced by pretrial treatment and supervision. Under most circumstances diversion programming would still provide a means for the defendant to work with his counsel in preparation of a defense and would not consist of the extensive controls existing in total confinement. However, one could easily hypothesize a situation where treatment programming could be as intense as incarceration, where the nature of the treatment would preclude the defendant from cooperating with counsel, and where the isolation of the defendant from his friends and relatives would be as complete as confinement itself. A relatively intrusive form of aversion therapy may well be more oppressive than confinement.

Anxiety and concern may or may not be minimized by diversion participation. Diversion increases the range of possible alternatives, which may increase the mental strain on defendants and their families. The anxiety over the outcome of a possible criminal trial remains. Added to this are the uncertainties of the outcome of the diversion program and its effect on the defendant as well as the strain of participation in treatment.

Delay in instituting criminal proceedings may burden the presentation of a defense. But in a particular case where delay will be a factor, the reason for the delay is immaterial. A defendant may make an eventual defense more difficult by participating in diversion and thereby postponing his trial.

This analysis suggests two potential points of concern in evaluating diversion programs. First, the defendant is confronted with difficult decisions involving his right to a speedy trial that may require the expert advice of counsel.[99] Second, given the flexible approach of the Court in *Barker* v. *Wingo*, the speedy-trial provision may put some outside limit on the length of diversion programming even where the defendant consents to the delay. The implicit coercion to participate by holding out the promise of dropping criminal charges in and of itself may not make a decision to participate involuntary. However, when combined with substantial pretrial delay it may invalidate the program on speedy-trial grounds.[100]

Notes

1. *See generally*, Skoler, *Protecting the Rights of Defendants in Pretrial Intervention Programs,* 10 CRIM. L. BULL. 473 (1974).

2. For federal statutes and programs, the guarantee of equal protection is inherent in the Fifth Amendment's due process clause.

3. *See* Yick Wo v. Hopkins, 118 U.S. 356 (1886).

4. For the analytic framework employed in the following discussion see generally, *Developments in the Law—Equal Protection*, 82 HARV. L. REV. 1065 (1969).

5. One frequently employed technique for narrowing the population of potential addict divertees is the practice of limiting participation to persons who have undergone treatment as a condition of pretrial release,

after arrest and arraignment but before consideration for diversion. It is a technique of classification that operates to exclude from consideration members of classes that may be defined as persons who refused to waive their Eighth Amendment rights to bail and persons who by reason of lack of funds have been detained in custody after arraignment. This subtle but nonetheless invidious discrimination directly affects the poor in their exercise of fundamental rights. It may well be that such criteria, if evaluated by the result of their application, may cause courts to apply a strict scrutiny test to equal protection challenges.

6. 414 U.S. 417 (1974).

7. Eligibility criteria based on the offense charged against the individual would seem difficult to justify. The fact that an addict–defendant is charged with shoplifting or prostitution rather than with possession or with breaking and entering rather than with shoplifting is best ascribed to the accidents of law enforcement. In the absence of evidence that the crime charged reveals anything of probable significance about the personality or criminal career of the accused, the constitutionality of an exclusionary classification based solely on the seriousness of a present charge is open to question. Since diversion may also be a new "track" within the criminal justice system, exclusion based on the seriousness of the offense charged seems particularly susceptible to constitutional challenge. *See, e.g.*, Rinaldi v. Yeager, 384 U.S. 305 (1966).

8. *Supra* note 6.

9. 18 U.S.C. § 4251 et seq. (1970); 28 U.S.C. § 2901 et seq. (1970); 42 U.S.C. § 3411 et seq. (1970).

10. 18 U.S.C. § 4251 (f) defines "eligible offender" to exclude among others, "an offender who is convicted of a crime of violence" and "an offender who has been convicted of a felony on two or more prior occasions."

11. 28 U.S.C. § 2901 et seq. (1966).

12. Marshall v. United States, 414 U.S. 417, 425 (1974).

13. *Id.*

14. *Id.* at 428, n. 11.

15. *Id.* at 428.

16. *Id.* at 429.

17. *Id.*

18. *Id.* at 429–30.

19. The hypothetical used by Justice Marshall dramatizes his disagreement with the two-felony exclusion. He notes that as written the statute would forbid Defendant *B*, who had two prior felony convictions for narcotic offenses, from receiving rehabilitative treatment but would allow Defendant *A*, who had previously been convicted of assault with in-

tent to commit murder, to enter the treatment program. ". . . one would think that Defendant *B*, all of whose criminal activity was related to his narcotics addiction, would be eligible for NARA treatment, while Defendant *A*, none of whose criminal activity was so related, would not be eligible. But just the opposite is true, because of the two-felony exclusion." *Id.* at 434 (Marshall, J. dissenting).

20. *Id.* at 424 n. 7.

21. *See generally,* M. FRANKEL, CRIMINAL SENTENCES: LAW WITHOUT ORDER (1973).

22. *See* pg. 56, *infra.*

23. Recent cases examining the constitutionality of conditions in pretrial detention facilities lend substantial support to the idea that persons accused of crime but not yet convicted must be treated differently than those already convicted. Indeed, some courts considering the rights of pretrial detainees have indicated they retain all rights of free citizens except those necessarily abridged to assure attendance at trial or the security of the detention facility. Rhen v. Malcolm, 371 F. Supp. 594, 623 (S.D. N.Y. 1974) (containing a review of earlier decisions involving pretrial detention).

24. 439 F.2d 442 (D.C. Cir. 1970) (en banc).

25. *See, e.g.,* Meyers v. United States, 388 F.2d 307 (9th Cir. 1968) (question of applicability of two-felony rule is "procedural" only.)

26. *See, e.g.,* United States v. Williams, 442 F.2d 738 (D.C. Cir. 1970); Chicquelo v. United States, 452 F.2d 1310 (D.C. Cir. 1971); Brooks v. United States, 457 F.2d 970 (9th Cir. 1972); United States v. Gillespie, 345 F. Supp. 1236 (W.D. Mo. 1972).

27. *See, e.g.,* Macias v. United States, 464 F.2d 1292 (5th Cir. 1972) (interpreting but not following *Watson.*)

28. 462 F.2d 1190 (D.C. Cir. 1972).

29. This reading, which turns on the proposition that the enactment of NARA reduced "the likelihood that an addict will get two felony convictions," 462 F.2d at 1193, was suggested by a footnote to the original *Watson* opinion. The court in *Hamilton* expressly declined to decide whether an exclusionary policy looking to post-1966 felony convictions would pass constitutional muster.

30. 470 F.2d 34 (9th Cir. 1972), *aff'd,* 414 U.S. 417 (1974).

31. 469 F.2d 1337 (1st Cir. 1972).

32. Smith v. Follette, 445 F.2d 955 (2d Cir. 1971), another decision rejecting the authority of *Watson,* is not on point. A challenge not to NARA, but to provisions of the New York Mental Hygiene Law, which made rehabilitative sentencing mandatory for convicted addict–misdemeanants but discretionary in the cases of addict–felons, *Smith*

did not deal with the problem of mandatory or automatic exclusionary criteria. Thus, it has no direct significance in an assessment of the constitutionality of the prior record bar in addict diversion.

33. 470 F.2d at 38–39.

34. 469 F.2d at 1340–1341.

35. *Id.* at 1343.

36. *Id.* at 1344.

37. *Id.* at 1345.

38. *Id.*

39. *See, e.g.*, Johnson v. Branch, 364 F.2d 177 (4th Cir. 1966), *cert. denied*, 385 U.S. 1003 (1967); Chambers v. Hendersonville City Board of Education, 364 F.2d 189 (4th Cir. 1966).

40. In its Supreme Court brief in the *Marshall* case, the government noted that the "optimum capacity" of the Bureau of Prisons' NARA II facilities was 600.

41. The recent case, Richardson v. Ramirez, 418 U.S. 24 (1974), is not applicable to this discussion. In *Richardson* the Court upheld the disenfranchisement of ex-felons but did so on the basis of the second clause of the Fourteenth Amendment which, to the majority, indicated the framers did not intend to deprive the states of the power to disenfranchise persons convicted of crime. It is significant that the Court did not consider the question under the equal protection clause, and thus the case is not authority for any deprivation imposed on convicted persons other than disenfranchisement.

42. *See, e.g.*, Duncan v. Louisiana, 391 U.S. 145 (1968).

43. 406 U.S. 356 (1972).

44. In order to "facilitate, expedite, and reduce expense in the administration of criminal justice, Louisiana has permitted less serious crimes to be tried by five jurors with unanimous verdicts, more serious crimes have required the assent of nine of 12 jurors, and for the most serious crimes a unanimous verdict of 12 jurors is stipulated. . . . We discern nothing invidious in this classification. . . . Appellant nevertheless insists that dispensing with unanimity in his case disadvantaged him as compared with those who commit less serious or capital crimes. With respect to the latter he is correct. . . . But as we have indicated, this does not constitute a denial of equal protection of the law; the State may treat capital offenders differently without violating the rights of those charged with lesser crime." *Id.* at 364.

45. 351 U.S. 12 (1956).

46. *See, e.g.*, Williams v. Oklahoma City, 395 U.S. 458 (1969) (denial of "case-made" to convicted ordinance violator); Roberts v. LaVallee,

389 U.S. 40 (1967) (denial of transcript of habeas corpus proceeding);
Draper v. Washington, 372 U.S. 487 (1963) (denial of trial transcript);
Douglas v. California, 372 U.S. 353 (1963) (denial of appointed appellate
counsel); Smith v. Bennett, 365 U.S. 708 (1961) (filing fee for state habeas
corpus petition); Burns v. Ohio, 360 U.S. 252 (1959) (filing fee for criminal appeal).

47. 384 U.S. 305, 310 (1966).

48. 411 U.S. 1, 102 (1972).

49. *Id.* at 29.

50. *See generally, Developments in the Law—Equal Protection*, 82 HARV.
L. REV. 1065, 1122–23 (1969). One such restriction would be a limitation
on participation in diversion to alleged offenders financially able to make
restitution to their purported victims.

51. For the view that the strictly dichotomized approach to equal protection analysis is in decline, *see* Note, *The Decline and Fall of the New
Equal Protection: A Polemical Approach*, 58 VA. L. REV. 1489 (1972). Professor Gerald Gunther, in *The Supreme Court, 1971 Term—Forward: In Search
of Evolving Doctrine on a Changing Court: A Model for a Newer Equal Protection*, 86 HARV. L. REV. 1 (1972), has explored the shape that a new equal
protection test based on an assessment of the appropriateness of means to
ends might take.

52. *For example, see* the description of a TASC (Treatment Alternatives to Street Crime) addict-diversion program contained in a "how-to"
manual distributed by the Law Enforcement Assistance Administration
to assist local agencies in establishing such programs. After wide-scale addict testing the description continues:

The judiciary then determines whether to send the arrestee to detention or to set
treatment as a condition of release and refer him to the TASC system. . . . If the
latter process is followed, an arrestee currently dependent on heroin is escorted to
a drug diagnostic unit for evaluation. . . . The individual continues treatment in
this facility subject to the standards and requirements of that treatment program.
During the treatment period, a tracking system functions to ensure that each
client is following conditions set at arraignment. This system reports drop-outs
from treatment or failure to comply with release conditions to the judiciary which
proceeds to handle the individual as if he had violated conditions of bail. When
the individual case comes to trial, the judiciary will take into account the addict's
cooperation and success in the treatment program thus far, and may determine
that he should remain in that program as an alternative to prosecution or possible
incarceration subsequent to prosecution.

LEAA, Guidlines for the Development of a Treatment, Alternatives to
Street Crime Project 7-8 (June 1973).

If, in fact, diversion programs are operated as described, the scrutiny due eligibility requirements becomes more urgent. If as suggested persons accused of crime are given the opportunity through pretrial treatment to better their chances of posttrial release, then those made ineligible for diversion because of some arbitrary criteria suffer direct consequences affecting their liberty.

53. One of the recurring problems in identifying candidates for diversion is the evaluation of individual "motivation." If a large number of addict–defendants are released on treatment-conditioned bond, the smaller number who are personally motivated to succeed in treatment can be selected out on the basis of their individual treatment histories, rather than by subjective prospective evaluation.

54. Whether or not knowledge of a defendant's drug-use history justifies the imposition of especially stringent release conditions or even the outright denial of bail—questions considered below—it is settled that the Eighth Amendment forbids setting money bail in amounts that individual defendants cannot meet solely as a device to insure their continued detention. *See, e.g.*, United States v. Motlow, 10 F.2d 657, 659 (7th Cir. 1926). In practice, however, such judicial manipulation of the money bond system usually is difficult to detect and impossible to control.

55. FREED & WALD, BAIL IN THE UNITED STATES (1964); U.S. PRESIDENT'S COMMISSION ON LAW ENFORCEMENT AND ADMINISTRATION OF JUSTICE, TASK FORCE REPORT: THE COURTS (1967); NATIONAL ADVISORY COMMISSION ON CRIMINAL JUSTICE STANDARDS AND GOALS, TASK FORCE REPORT: CORRECTIONS (1972); ABA STANDARDS, PRETRIAL RELEASE (1968).

56. This is the express constitutional or statutory rule for noncapital cases in an overwhelming majority of the states and in the federal courts under Rule 43 of the Federal Rules of Civil Procedure. The question as to whether the Eighth Amendment, in itself, implies an absolute right to bail in noncapital cases remains unresolved. *Compare* Foote, *The Coming Constitutional Crisis in Bail*: I, 113 U. PA. L. REV. 959 (1965), and Meyer, *Constitutionality of Pretrial Detention*, 60 GEO. L. J. 1140 (1972).

57. This is the rule for felony cases under New York law as now interpreted. *See, e.g.*, People v. Melville, 62 Misc.2d 366, 308 N.Y.S.2d 671 (Crim. Ct. 1970).

58. Although the United States Supreme Court has not ruled that the bail clause of the Eighth Amendment is directly applicable to states through the Fourteenth Amendment, state constitutional provisions themselves supply their own prohibitions against the requirement of excessive bail.

59. *See*, Stack v. Boyle, 342 U.S. 1 (1951). It is, indeed, troubling that the Law Enforcement Assistance Administration's "how-to" booklet on establishing an addict-diversion program comes close to recommending

that bail be used to facilitate the administration of the diversion program in ways that could have no relationship to any of the asserted purposes of bail. Consider the following instruction for program planners:

> One problem likely to occur in the lock-up procedure is a high proportion of missed interviews due to the quick release of the arrestee on his own recognizance or by making bail. This problem can be solved several ways. First, the interviewer must make every effort to contact the arrestee as soon as he is available. Secondly, the person taking custody of the arrestee released on O.R. may encourage the arrestee to complete the interview if he understands the nature of the TASC program. Thirdly, the bench may be persuaded to insist on a completed interview, including urinalysis, as a pre-condition of bail. Fourthly, the bench might increase the bail if he feels the arrestee, as a possible addict, might endanger the community.

LEAA, Guidelines for the Development of a Treatment Alternatives to Street Crime Project, 64 (June 1973). The third approach to this "problem" if it results in detention for a longer period than would otherwise be the case would seriously conflict with the excessive bail restriction. Implicit in the suggestion is that regardless of a person's eligibility for pretrial release immediately, the release should be delayed in order to facilitate the administration of a program.

Another problem is foreseen by program planners:

> Several problem areas here should be identified and dealt with as quickly as possible:
> ... 3) A large number of clients leaving TASC during or immediately after detoxification due to the bench's setting treatment as a condition of relatively low bail. The bail is high enough to force the client into limited treatment, but low enough for him to acquire the money before he has a chance to become enmeshed in a good program. ...

Id. at 75–76. Of course the implication is that the judge determined that the "low" bail was sufficient for the purposes of the bail system suggesting that bail higher than otherwise required would be useful for purposes of diversion programming.

60. *See, e.g.,* Mitchell, *Bail Reform and the Constitutionality of Pretrial Detention,* 55 VA. L. REV. 1223 (1969). The District of Columbia has a preventative detention statute. D.C. Code § 23-1322 (1973). The provision was upheld. Blunt v. United States, 322 A.2d 579 (D.C. Ct. App. 1974). The court, however, dealt with a case where the defendant had threatened the lives of witnesses against him and held that courts have authority to detain in order to protect witnesses. The case cannot be considered a carte blanche approval of preventive detention statutes, particularly where the detention does not seek to prevent danger to others but is used as a device to insure treatment for the person detained.

61. Two contractors for the Special Action Office for Drug Abuse Prevention hired to study the legal implications of addict-diversion programs came to opposite conclusions regarding the Eighth Amendment and its applicability to diversion programs. TASC Legal Analysis (Sept. 1973).

62. For two recent cases see In Re Underwood, 9 Cal.3d 345, 508 P.2d 721, 107 Cal. Rptr. 401 (1973); Martin v. State, 517 P.2d 1389 (Alaska 1974).

63. The indirect relevance of possible future criminal activity to the likelihood of flight has been recognized by courts that otherwise bar the consideration of risk to the community alone as a factor in the bail decision. *See, e.g.*, Commonwealth v. Truesdale, 449 Pa. 325, 296 A.2d 829 (1972).

64. *See*, D.C. CODE § 23-1322 (1973); ALASKA STAT. ANN. 12.30.020 (a) (Mitchie 1972). The Alaska provision was limited by the Alaska Supreme Court to confer power on the trial courts to consider "dangerousness" in fixing the amount of bail or the conditions of bail but not to deny bail altogether. Martin v. State, 517 P.2d 1389 (Alaska 1974).

65. For the general proposition that drug dependence is relevant to the issue of dangerousness as applied in particular cases involving denial of postconviction appeal bonds, *see, e.g.*, United States v. Turner, 470 F.2d 372 (D.C. Cir. 1972); United States v. Bond, 329 F. Supp. 538 (E.D. Tenn. 1971).

66. U.S. PRESIDENT'S COMMISSION ON LAW ENFORCEMENT AND ADMINISTRATION OF JUSTICE, TASK FORCE REPORT: NARCOTICS AND DRUG ABUSE (1967).

67. This assumes that the jurisdiction in question has not barred its courts from imposing nonmonetary conditions of pretrial release in addition to, or as a substitute for, monetary bail. Although the power to use some nonmonetary conditions, for example, restrictions on travel and association, would appear to be inherent in the courts, see Brown v. Fogel, 387 F.2d 692 (4th Cir. 1967), additional statutory authorization may be required before more specialized conditions, such as those requiring drug treatment can be imposed. The Federal Courts have sufficient authority under provisions of the Federal Bail Reform Act of 1966, 18 U.S.C. § 3141 et. seq. (1970). *See also* NATIONAL ADVISORY COMMISSION ON CRIMINAL JUSTICE STANDARDS AND GOALS, TASK FORCE REPORT: CORRECTIONS, Std. 4.4 (1973).

68. The Federal Bail Reform Act, *supra* note 67, requires the court to impose the least restrictive condition necessary to assure the accused's presence at trial. The American Bar Association has also recommended this approach. See ABA STANDARDS, PRETRIAL RELEASE § 5.2 (1968). See also, NATIONAL COMMISSION ON CRIMINAL JUSTICE STANDARDS AND GOALS, CORRECTIONS, Std. 4.4 (1973).

69. 18 U.S.C. § 3146 et seq. (1970).

70. 451 F.2d 1198 (5th Cir. 1971).

71. In *Cramer* the defendant was a college student of 19, and the supplementary conditions initially imposed by the trial court were of an essentially paternalistic character. The Court of Appeals noted, however, that the trial court's motives were irrelevant to the question of whether such conditions were necessary to provide reasonable assurance that the defendant would appear.

72. *See, e.g.,* Long v. Hamilton, 467 S.W.2d 139 (Ky. Ct. of App. 1971) ($150,000 bail excessive); Matera v. Buchanan, 192 So.2d 18 (Fla. D. Ct. App. 1966) ($250,000 bail excessive).

73. *See generally* Note, *Constitutional Limitations on the Conditions of Pretrial Detention,* 79 YALE L.J. 941 (1970); NATIONAL ADVISORY COMMISSION ON CRIMINAL JUSTICE STANDARDS AND GOALS, CORRECTIONS, Std. 4.8 (1972).

74. In recent cases involving pretrial detainees, the courts have begun to recognize that *detention* conditions must be limited by those necessary to assure the presence of the accused at trial. In Rhem v. Malcolm, 371 F. Supp. 594 (S.D.N.Y. 1974), Judge Lasker in finding the New York pretrial detention facility, known as "the tombs," seriously deficient held: "These propositions are now firmly embedded in the law: That a detainee may not be deprived of the rights of other citizens beyond the extent necessary to assure his appearance at trial and the security of the institution to which he is confined." *Id.* at 623. And see Seale v. Manson, 326 F. Supp. 1375 (D. Conn. 1971), cited by Judge Lasker, in which the court held that conditions of pretrial detention must relate to security and that "considerations of rehabilitation, deterrence, or punishment are not material." *Id.* at 1379. While these cases involve problems of cruel and unusual punishment and due process, they serve as support for defining "excessive bail in the context of nonmonetary conditions of pretrial release.

75. Whether a drug-related condition directly achieves participation in treatment or merely commands abstinence and directs that the defendant appear for periodic urinalysis, fulfilling the directive of the court will necessarily require a considerable disruption of the defendant's ordinary routine; by necessity, compliance with a drug-related condition entails frequent attendance at a clinic or screening facility and the loss of considerable time and freedom of movement. In addition, required urinalysis raises Fourth Amendment problems.

76. The issue of drug-related conditions cannot be totally separated from bail practices regarding nonaddict arrestees. A policy using drug-related conditions in lieu of monetary release for addicts but relying solely on monetary bail for nonaddicts might be challenged by nonaddicts as

violations of their equal protection and due process interests. At the same time, addicts might challenge such a procedure arguing that they are subjected to greater restrictions than nonaddicts.

77. *Compare*, United States v. Alston, 420 F.2d 176 (D.C. Cir. 1969) (order setting conditions of pretrial release including participation in alcoholic rehabilitation program); Stinnett v. United States, 387 F.2d 238 (D.C. Cir. 1967) (order remanding case of pretrial detainee for consideration of release conditions adapted to his problem of mental illness); *and* Vauss v. United States, 365 F.2d 956 (D.C. Cir. 1966) (bail pending appeal refused to known narcotic addict that no program for treatment of surveillance existed to which he could be required to report two or three times weekly).

78. *See* Ackies v. Purdy, 322 F. Supp. 38 (S.D. Fla. 1970) (practice of setting monetary conditions of release by reference to "master bond schedule" violated equal protection of Fourteenth Amendment by denying right to pretrial release on reasonable conditions).

79. It is generally agreed that persons not under state control may refuse "treatment" except in the most extraordinary circumstances where the lack of treatment represents a clear danger to others. *See, e.g.*, Jacobson v. Massachusetts, 197 U.S. 11 (1905) upholding mandatory smallpox vaccinations under epidemic conditions. A free citizen's right of privacy emanating from such cases as Stanley v. Georgia, 394 U.S. 557 (1969), and Griswold v. Connecticut, 381 U.S. 479 (1965), protects him from imposed treatment. Even where the state exercises some control over an individual the courts are divided on the extent to which involuntary treatment can be imposed. *See generally* Note, *Conditioning and Other Technologies Used to "Treat?" "Rehabilitate?" "Demolish?" Prisoners and Mental Patients*, 45 So. Cal. Rev. 616 (1972).

80. Rhem v. Malcolm, 371 F. Supp. 594 (S.D.N.Y. 1974). See *id.* at 624, n. 5 for the court's discussion of the appropriate constitutional provision used to prohibit forced treatment of pretrial detainees.

81. Such an attempt to exact a waiver of the right to privacy would be obviously impermissible if the offense charged were bailable as a matter of constitutional right in the jurisdiction in question. It is axiomatic that the exercise of one secured right cannot be made to depend on the forfeiture of another. It should be deemed equally offensive, however, if admission to pretrial release is merely discretionary in a particular case. A mere "privilege" may be as precious in practice as a "right"; the privilege of release on bail is an obvious example. *See generally* Rankin, *The Effect of Pretrial Detention*, 39 N.Y.U.L. Rev. 631 (1964). The denial of a mere privilege may be as impermissible a device for coercing the waiver of constitutional guarantees as the denial of a right. *See generally* Van Alstyne,

The Demise of the Right-Privilege Distinction in Constitutional Law, 81 HARV. L. REV. 1439 (1968).

82. The Fourth Amendment objections to mandatory urinalysis following arrest, discussed at pg. 16, *supra,* must be reexamined in the context of a conditional release. It could be argued that in this latter context, the search is a consent search since the arrestee can always refuse the condition if he desires to remain detained awaiting trial. The issues raised here have not been extensively litigated. In People v. Bremmer, 30 Cal. App.3d 1058, 106 Cal. Rptr. 797 (2d Dist. Ct. App. 1973), a condition of probation subjecting the probationer to a general search without a warrant by any peace officer was deemed to be unreasonable and void. The court authorized searches without warrant by probation officers at any time and other law enforcement officers only on reasonable suspicion justifying the search. *See also* In re Marks, 71 Cal. 2d 31, 77 Cal. Rptr. 1, 453 P.2d 441 (1969) (approving regular and surprise testing of state commitment program outpatients).

83. A program that offers drug-dependent defendants a single form of treatment as an alternative to detention runs a greater risk of constitutional attack, particularly where the one form of treatment is relatively intrusive such as methadone maintenance. *See generally* Note, *Methadone Maintenance for Heroin Addicts,* 78 YALE L.J. 1175 (1969).

84. *See* Skoler, *Protecting the Rights of Defendants in Pretrial Intervention Programs,* 10 CRIM. L. BULL. 473 (1974).

85. The effect of the guilty plea in diversion programs is not adequately explained in the descriptive literature. A number of possibilities exist; the critical question is whether the guilty plea will subsequently be used against the defendant in a trial. In some diversion programs participation in treatment occurs while the process of prosecution continues, the only benefit to participation being the consideration given to treatment progress at sentencing. In these programs a guilty plea could be the basis for conviction. In programs deferring prosecution, the guilty plea could be used in one of three ways: the plea remains of record during the diversion program but is withdrawn and expunged on termination of treatment whether successful or not; the plea is used as an admission against interest when prosecution is resumed although the person is allowed to withdraw the plea; or the plea remains should treatment fail as the basis for imposition of sentence.

86. Boykin v. Alabama, 395 U.S. 238 (1969).

87. 390 U.S. 570 (1968).

88. 397 U.S. 742 (1970).

89. The plea in Brady was entered prior to the *Jackson* decision.

90. 400 U.S. 25 (1970).

91. *Id.* at 31.

92. Rule 11 of the Federal Rules of Criminal Procedure requires the court approve a guilty plea only after personally addressing the defendant and "determining that the plea is made voluntarily with understanding of the nature of the charge and the consequences of the plea." This has been held to be a mandatory provision, with which failure to comply invalidated the plea. McCarthy v. United States, 394 U.S. 459 (1969). *See also* Boykin v. Alabama, 395 U.S. 238 (1969) (record must disclose plea is voluntary).

93. The implications of the guilty plea requirement for the right to counsel is considered, *infra.*

94. 397 U.S. at 752.

95. *Id.* at 758.

96. Klopfer v. North Carolina, 386 U.S. 213 (1967).

97. United States v. Marion, 404 U.S. 307 (1971). *Marion* also recognizes a general due process right to be free from unconscionable delay prior to the initiation of formal proceedings.

98. 407 U.S. 514 (1972).

99. The right to counsel in the diversion context is considered in chapter 4, *infra.*

100. Speedy trial and general due process may be the only protection against unreasonable delay. The statute of limitations could be easily satisfied by filing formal charges. There are some circumstances that might suggest a due process challenge. For example, a troubling possibility would exist where the length of the treatment program exceeded the maximum sentence for the offense underlying the defendant's arrest. Also, the continuance of a defendant in a program that offers little chance of success may be similarly objectionable. *See* Jackson v. Indiana, 406 U.S. 715 (1972), in which the Court freed an accused who had been committed as incompetent to stand trial. Justice Blackmun, in an unanimous opinion, reasoned that due process required that the state show that continued commitment serves the state interest in improving the competency of the individual to stand trial.

4 The Right to Counsel

As we have seen from the preceding discussion, the early procedures of an addict-diversion program confront a pretrial detainee with various options, many of which directly affect his constitutional rights. Indeed, many of the decisions he must make and many of the governmental actions that may be taken with regard to him may seriously affect any subsequent determination of his guilt or innocence or substantially affect any sentence imposed. The criminal justice system relies on representation by counsel as a means of insuring that a person accused of crime can adequately defend himself and intelligently respond to the numerous choices presented to him.

The "right to counsel" comes from several sources and its application at various stages of a criminal case is still the subject of dispute. The Sixth Amendment insures the assistance of counsel "in all criminal prosecutions," which requires a definition of "criminal prosecution." The Supreme Court has also indicated that in certain situations where other constitutional rights are in jeopardy, the presence of counsel may be an important or a determining factor in whether a waiver is voluntary. Since addict diversion raises a variety of different constitutional problems the presence of counsel at each stage of the diversion program must be considered.

The Sixth Amendment

The Supreme Court long ago recognized that the Sixth Amendment, which provides the right of counsel in all criminal prosecutions, was not limited in application to the trial itself. Trial counsel may be rendered ineffective by decisions and events prior to the trial, and thus the Court has consistently required representation at all "critical stages."[1] In a series of cases the Court extended the definition of critical stage to include preliminary hearings, arraignments, and other situations in which the defendant could benefit from legal advice. Perhaps the high water mark of this extension was *United States* v. *Wade*[2] and *Gilbert* v. *California*.[3] These two cases held that a postindictment lineup in which the defendant is identified by witnesses is a critical confrontation subject to the Sixth Amendment.

The recent retreat from this pinnacle began with *Kirby* v. *Illinois*,[4] in which the Court limited *Wade* and *Gilbert* to events occurring after "formal charges, preliminary hearing, indictment, information, or arraignment." In a plurality opinion Mr. Justice Stewart noted that these procedures mark the "starting point for our whole system of adversary criminal justice . . . [and] it is only than that the Government has committed itself to prosecute. . . ."[5] Specifically, the Court held that counsel was not required at a lineup conducted prior to this starting point. The view of the majority of the court is not clear, however, since only four justices joined in Stewart's opinion. The critical fifth vote was that of Justice Powell who concurred in the result because he did not want to extend the per se exclusionary rule of *Wade* and *Gilbert*. Whether he was concerned with the existence of the right to counsel or merely with the remedy remains ambiguous. In any event, *Kirby*, for all its ambiguity, attempts to delineate the point at which a prosecution commences.

The most recent attempt at defining the limits of the Sixth Amendment failed to provide any more definitive parameter to the problem or any clearer understanding of the view of the swing Justices. In *United States* v. *Ash*,[6] in a 6–3 opinion, Justice Blackmun found the Sixth Amendment inapplicable to a postindictment display of photographs to witnesses. Justice White, who dissented in *Kirby* on the basis of *Wade* and *Gilbert*, silently joined the majority in *Ash*. Justice Powell similarly added his vote without comment. Only Justice Stewart, who had written *Kirby*, felt compelled to offer a concurring opinion.

In *Ash* the display of photographs to witnesses occurred after indictment and was thus clearly within the "prosecution" as defined in *Kirby*. The Court concentrated on providing a definition of "critical stage." The majority recognized two interests thought to be served by counsel in pretrial proceedings: (a) the interest of the defendant in receiving assistance on complex legal issues, and (b) the need to protect the accused against "overreaching" by the prosecutor by minimizing the imbalance that would result if the government were represented by counsel and the accused were not. *Wade* was interpreted as suggesting that the nature of a lineup and the scientific imprecision that may result could not be cured at trial through cross-examination, and thus the lineup was "critical." A contrary result would not protect the accused from prosecutorial overreaching. The reliability of the photographic display in *Ash*, however, could be tested at trial and thus was not a "critical stage." Justice Stewart, while agreeing with the conclusion, indicated that in his view the only interest for providing counsel at pretrial proceedings was to insure the ultimate effectiveness of counsel at the trial.

This review of recent Sixth Amendment cases sets the stage for consideration of the application of the right to counsel in diversion procedures. The inquiry must focus on two issues: (1) when does the "prosecution" begin within the *Kirby* decision, and (2) what procedures subsequent to the initiation of the prosecution are "critical stages" as defined by *Ash?*

The Commencement of the Prosecution

A strict reading of *Kirby* can support the proposition that a prosecution cannot commence under any circumstances until the intervention of the judiciary either through the filing of formal charges or the initiation of judicial proceedings such as arraignment. If this interpretation is the correct one, many of the early identification procedures associated with diversion programs would fall outside Sixth Amendment protection. Programs that conduct urinalysis and drug-use interviews immediately after arrest would avoid, at least for Sixth Amendment purposes, a requirement of counsel.

On the other hand, it seems largely mechanistic to ascribe that interpretation to *Kirby*. The events that would trigger the Sixth Amendment are largely in the control of the prosecution. While it may well be that the Sixth Amendment counsel provision was not intended to be directly applicable to the investigative stage of a criminal case, it is possible that the prosecution can commit itself to prosecute and solidify its position while artificially postponing the initiation of formal charges. It is doubtful that the Court would validate such actions.[7]

Diversion programs are constructed in a variety of ways regarding the stage of the proceeding in which a person may be diverted or, more importantly, considered for diversion. Many are postarraignment diversions in which formal judicial intervention precedes diversionary treatment. In others, formal charges are not filed nor indictment sought until after the community program is completed. There does not appear to be any compelling reason why any particular point in the proceeding would be selected for diversion. While diversion prior to the filing of formal charges may avoid a requirement that the court participate in the diversion decision, some programs diverting prior to formal charging give the judge a voice in the decision. The decision to divert will in part be based on the offense thought to have been committed by the accused. Thus the initiation of the diversion decision-making process in and of itself indicates in most cases that the "investigatory" stage has ended and that the prosecution has "focused" on the accused. Seen in this light, the *Kirby* requirement of "commencement" may be met even in some precharge-diversion programs.

The *Kirby* demarcation would include within a "criminal prosecution" all diversion-related activities occurring after formal charges are filed. Thus in programs where the decision to divert is made after formal charging, the accused has the right to the assistance of counsel. However, even in such programs the investigation of persons to determine their eligibility for diversion may take place before that time. Urinalysis and drug-use interviews may occur shortly after arrest. *Kirby* thus raises a substantial hurdle for asserting the right to have counsel present during these activities at least as far as the Sixth Amendment is concerned.

Kirby, however, can be distinguished from cases involving addict-identification procedures. In *Kirby* the focus of the investigation was still on whether the defendant had in fact committed the offense. The underlying assumption of *Kirby* is the protection of society's interest in allowing police to carry on an investigation unimpeded by the intervention of counsel. Accepting that interest as dispositive, it remains inapplicable in the diversion context. The investigation here is not on who committed what offense but whether the person is eligible for treatment. Society's interest in the capture of offenders is no longer at stake. Its interest is limited to the timing of the imposition of treatment—whether prior to or subsequent to conviction. Since pretrial diversion appears to be a benefit to the accused, it is doubtful that counsel would intentionally impede such an investigation. Yet, it is the seeming beneficience of the program that increases the need for counsel to prevent an accused, in the rush to avoid prosecution, from foregoing the legal protection to which he is entitled.

The Critical Stage

Assuming that some activities in the diversion context occur after the initiation of a "criminal prosecution," the recent Supreme Court decision in *United States* v. *Ash* requires consideration of whether an activity represents a "critical stage" and thus requires the presence of counsel. In *Ash* photographs of the accused were shown witnesses after indictment but prior to trial. The Court held that counsel was not required at this photographic display. The "critical stage" of a prosecution was limited to "trial-like confrontations" in which the interests served by the Sixth Amendment are in jeopardy.

The *Ash* decision should not represent a substantial obstacle to asserting a Sixth Amendment right to counsel in diversion proceedings since in diversion programs the Sixth Amendment interests are involved and their advancement requires the appointment of counsel. In *Ash* the defendant was not present and was thus not confronted with any legal decision requiring assistance. As indicated throughout this work, the person subject to the actions of diversion staff is faced with complex legal dilemmas that can only be intelligently resolved with the help of an attorney. Similarly in *Ash* the counsel at trial could at least pursue the accuracy of the identification procedures and challenge the credibility of the witness. In the diversion context the decisions may well preclude a trial or seriously undermine a defense should a trial occur. Thus the effectiveness of counsel at trial is at stake in early diversion proceedings, and the opportunity for prosecutorial overreaching is a real one.

Counsel and Waiver of Other Rights

In addition to the Sixth Amendment guarantee of the right to counsel in criminal prosecutions, the presence of counsel has been required at points outside the "criminal prosecution" when other constitutional rights are in jeopardy. Counsel is seen as one device to insure that a waiver of another constitutional right is voluntary and based on an intelligent appraisal of the probable results. To determine at what stage in a diversion program counsel must be available requires a separate analysis of the various other rights which must be waived in the process.

Drug-use Interviews

In *Miranda* v. *Arizona*[8] the Court held that an accused subject to police interrogation in custody must be advised of his right to an attorney prior to such interrogation. The right to representation in this situation is designed to protect the Fifth Amendment privilege against self-incrimination. The Court recognized that interrogation in the custodial surroundings of the police station is so inherently coercive that the presence of counsel is necessary. Since drug-use interviews would most likely be conducted in custody, *Miranda* would appear to require counsel if requested by the person to be interviewed. Furthermore, the interviewer would be obligated to warn the accused that he has the right to counsel.

Since the presence of counsel in these circumstances after *Kirby* is limited to protecting the privilege aganist self-incrimination, the extent to which the Fifth Amendment privilege is compromised will determine the requirement for counsel. As discussed earlier, a grant of total-use immunity for statements made during the interview would eliminate not only the problem of self-incrimination but would also alleviate the need for counsel.[9]

Urinalysis

Urinalysis testing calls into question the applicability of the Fourth Amendment. A search pursuant to a judicial warrant does not require the presence of counsel. The Supreme Court has not required counsel to advise a person on whether he should consent to a search. However, there are suggestions in some cases that make the presence of counsel prior to urinalysis a possible requirement.

The most recent case involving consent searches would seem to negate a requirement of counsel. In *Schneckloth* v. *Bustamonte*,[10] the Supreme Court refused to require the police to advise the subject of a search of his right to withhold his consent to the search. Arguably such a requirement would be more easily imposed than a requirement that counsel be present. However, the search in *Schneckloth* was not a search conducted on a person in full custody. In diversion programs urinalysis would be conducted in the custodial surroundings of the police station or lockup, and many of the coercive features that troubled the courts in the confession cases leading to *Miranda* would be present.[11]

In *Gilbert* v. *California*,[12] the Supreme Court specifically held that counsel was not required at the taking of handwriting exemplars. Two factors serve to distinguish *Gilbert*. First, handwriting exemplars are not covered by the Fourth Amendment while the privacy interest is involved in urinalysis testing situations.[13] In *Gilbert* the accused did not have to evaluate whether to give his consent since the exemplar could be taken involuntarily. The Court in *Gilbert* also noted that the accused could protect himself against an unrepresentative sample by providing additional samples at the trial. Thus, his opportunity for cross-examination and rebuttal were preserved. In urinalysis, however, this opportunity is lost with the sample taken. The presence of counsel is needed to insure the accuracy of the sample, the appropriateness of the conditions under which it is taken, and the voluntariness of the consent.

In *Schmerber* v. *California*,[14] where the Court upheld the taking of a blood sample from an unconsenting driver, the Court recognized that the driver did have counsel present at the time of the sampling. Thus, assuming the Fourth Amendment does not prohibit the taking, the reasonableness of the search may be determined by the presence or absence of an attorney.

Guilty Pleas

Many diversion programs require a conditional plea of guilty prior to admission to the program. To do this, a period of negotiation must take place between the accused and representatives of the prosecution. This is "plea bargaining." We have considered earlier the difficult choices facing an accused when confronted with a guilty plea as the price for diversion. The most recent plea-bargaining cases, *Brady* v. *United States*,[15] and *North*

Carolina v. *Alford*,[16] have determined that pleas are voluntary even though entered to avoid the possibility of the death sentence.[17]

Whatever view one takes of the validity of the guilty plea requirement as a condition to diversion, it seems clear from all the cases that an accused is entitled to consult with counsel in considering the choice of pleading guilty. In most instances the plea itself will be made at a hearing at which counsel is required by the Sixth Amendment. Certainly the prosecution has focused sufficiently on the accused to require counsel during the negotiations, at least at the postcharge stage.

Both *Brady* and *Alford*, while not specifically holding that counsel is required at the negotiations, strongly suggest that to be the case. Emphasizing the difficult choice confronting the accused in those cases, the Court emphasized that in both the pleas were entered on the advice of competent counsel. It is strongly implicit in the opinions that the voluntariness of the plea would be seriously jeopardized if counsel were not available.

Speedy Trial

Participation in a diversion program necessarily requires the waiver of the defendant's right to a speedy trial. The Supreme Court has validated the voluntary waiver of this right and has proposed a balancing test to determine when the right has been waived.[18] One of the critical factors used by the Court in determining the voluntariness of the waiver or the deprivation of the right is whether counsel was available to advise the accused.

Conclusion

The above discussion has isolated the interests that would suggest a defendant faced with the prospects of diversion is entitled to the assistance of counsel. In each instance, taken separately, the cases do not provide a clear and adamant requirement of counsel. However, as each right subject to waiver is examined, it appears that counsel would add significantly to the fairness with which a diversion program operated. Taken together, the complexity and interrelationship of the rights and potentially beneficial alternatives opened to the defendant increase the need for the advice of counsel.

A useful role for professional legal counsel exists in the early stages of diversionary programming. As a source of advice to prospective participants concerning the pros and cons of the diversionary option, as an advocate in obtaining the best diversionary "deal" for the individual defendant and as a check against official overreaching, the defense lawyer can make positive contributions.

As the analysis just concluded shows, however, the basis for a general *right* to counsel at this stage of the process of addict diversion is less certain. In a "postcharge" diversion program, the arguments favoring a right to counsel at intake seem compelling; in a "precharge" program, they are relatively weak in light of *Kirby*. It remains for further litigation to clarify the nature of the divertee's right to counsel.

Notes

1. Powell v. Alabama, 287 U.S. 45 (1932).
2. 388 U.S. 218 (1967).
3. 388 U.S. 263 (1967).
4. 406 U.S. 682 (1972).
5. *Id.* at 689.
6. 413 U.S. 300 (1973).
7. Moore v. Oliver, 347 F. Supp. 1313 (W.D. Va. 1972): "In view of the wide diversity of state criminal practices, there may not be any magic words that delineate for all purposes what is and what is not a critical stage of the proceeding within the meaning of the Sixth Amendment" *Id.* at 1319. *See also* U.S. *ex. rel.* Robinson v. Zelker, 468 F.2d 159 (2d Cir. 1972), where a New York statute providing that a prosecution commenced upon issuance of an arrest warrant was used to require consel prior to formal charging.
8. 384 U.S. 436 (1966).
9. Of course it is possible for the diversion staff to continue to interview arrestees without counsel with the risk that the information would not be admissible in a subsequent trial. It is doubtful that prosecutors would support continued interviewing on this basis, and injunctive relief against systematic violations of the Fifth Amendment would be available.
10. 412 U.S. 218 (1973).
11. For a more detailed analysis see page 36, *supra*.
12. 388 U.S. 263 (1967).
13. See discussion page 17, *supra*.
14. 384 U.S. 757 (1966).
15. 397 U.S. 742 (1970).
16. 400 U.S. 25 (1970).
17. See page 64, *supra*, regarding the validity of the guilty plea requirement for diversion eligibility.
18. Barker v. Wingo, 407 U.S. 514 (1972).

5

The Role of the Prosecutor and Court in Diversion Programs

Both federal and state governments are divided into three separate branches, each with its own defined powers and responsibilities. The criminal justice system reflects this division of authority, and the legislature, courts, and executive participate at various stages of the criminal process. In a case that proceeds along the traditional track of the process, the limits of the powers of each branch are largely defined. However, in some programs, such as pretrial diversion, where the traditional functions merge, difficult legal issues regarding the appropriate decision maker are raised. In the few cases that have been litigated, the issues have been framed around whether one branch may veto or restrict the discretion of the other branch. Whether a particular branch has the authority to act in the first instance has not been generally considered. The scope of the power of the three branches in the diversion context will depend on varying interpretations of state and federal constitutional law and the statutory authority, if it exists, creating the diversion program. The following discussion analyzes the recent cases most directly related to sorting out the various governmental functions in the diversion context.

The Decision to Divert

The prosecutor has the discretion to bring or not to bring formal criminal charges against any alleged offender. The precise limits of this discretion have never been clearly defined. Courts, nevertheless, interpret this discretion broadly. The basic concept of the prosecutor's broad discretion in the charging function is well recognized.[1] Prosecutors have long engaged in large-scale diversion on an ad hoc informal basis.[2] A formal pretrial-diversion program standardizes this discretion through its rules, regulations, and eligibility criteria and exposes it to public view and understanding. The end goal is not one of expanding the scope of discretion, but of exercising it more intelligently and fairly.

As a practical matter, the court will not have a role in the initial decision to divert a particular offender if the diversion occurs prior to the initiation of formal charges. Until the judicial process is begun, courts will not be notified of the status of persons for whom diversion is a possible alternative. Thus, there appears no legal obstacle to development of a prosecutorial-diversion program where the decision to divert is made prior to charge. As long as the prosecutor retains the largely unlimited discretion to charge or not to charge, a program that systematizes the exercise of that discretion seems well within the range of his powers. Courts may become involved where a person against whom charges are brought seeks to challenge the prosecutorial decision not to divert. However, in the one analogous decision, the Wisconsin Supreme Court refused to review the prosecutor's decision.[3]

Postcharge diversion, occurring at or after arraignment, indictment, or charge by way of information, presents a more difficult problem. It brings into play both judicial and executive functions. It is a hybrid procedure not susceptible of traditional criminal-process categorization. Where intervention occurs after charges have formally been brought, the traditional prosecutorial function is only advisory to the judicial power of determining if prosecution is to be continued, deferred, or dismissed.

The prosecutor does control the initiation and prosecution of criminal cases. If a decision is made pursuant to pretrial-intervention criteria to divert an alleged offender, with the possibility of the dismissal of criminal charges, the prosecutor should arguably have more than an advisory function. Persons diverted have waived rights in reliance on future actions of the prosecutor.[4]

Final resolution of the court–prosecutor conflict of functions and interest must await further litigation. There is, however, some case law that may help to delineate the respective roles of the two branches in making the decision to divert, at least after formal charging. In *People* v. *Superior Court of San Mateo County*,[5] the California Supreme Court held that a statute providing a prosecutorial veto over a court's decision to divert a criminal defendant was unconstitutional as violating separation of powers. The case involved a diversion program created by legislation that gave the court the power to divert after formal charges were filed.

The court based its decision on a line of earlier opinions involving the demarcation of the prosecutor's powers. In *People* v. *Tenorio*,[6] the court had ruled invalid a legislative grant of power to the prosecutor to veto the trial judge's decision to award lenient sentences to convicted narcotics offenders with a prior criminal record. The court there noted:

[w]hen the decision to prosecute has been made, the process which leads to acquittal or to sentencing is fundamentally judicial in nature. . . . The judicial power is compromised when a judge, who believes that a charge should be dismissed in the interests of justice, wishes to exercise the power to dismiss but finds that before he may do so he must bargain with the prosecutor.[7]

In addition to *Tenorio*, the court had earlier struck down a prosecutorial veto of the civil commitment of a narcotics addict,[8] and a judicial determination that a charged offense be tried as a misdemeanor rather than a felony.[9] The court also relied on a lower court case invalidating the power of a prosecutor to veto probation.[10]

In the diversion case, the court noted that

... diversion may also be viewed as a specialized form of probation, available to a different class of defendants but sharing many similarities with general probation and commitment for addiction. Like those programs, diversion is intended to offer a second chance to offenders who are minimally involved in crime and maximally motivated to reform, and the decision to divert is predicated on an indepth appraisal of the background and personality of the particular individual before the court.[11]

In light of the substantial precedent on separation of powers available to the California Supreme Court, it is not surprising that it extended the judicial power to the diversion decision free of the fetters of the prosecutorial veto. It should be noted, however, that in many jurisdictions the courts have not been as solicitous of their power.[12]

In addition to the constitutional separation of power issue, diversion programs based on statutory authorization may raise difficult questions of the allocation of power. In a recent case, *United States* v. *Gillespie*,[13] a federal district court examined the use of Title III of the Narcotic Addict Rehabilitation Act[14] as a preindictment diversion mechanism for certain addicts under investigation in connection with federal offenses. Title III provides for the "civil" adjudication and commitment of narcotics addicts "not charged with any criminal offenses." The title has been employed in some federal districts to accomplish in practice the aims of pretrial diversion. An addict subject to potential prosecution will volunteer for NARA III commitment and, as the court in *Gillespie* explained:

In every NARA case processed in this district, save only this case, the United States Attorney's office has ... held every possible criminal charge in abeyance by simply determining that no criminal complaint should be filed or presented to a grand jury until after treatment under NARA may have failed.[15]

Significantly, the federal prosecutor is given by statute a central administrative role in any NARA III adjudication; it is the United States Attorney's Office that must petition the court, on behalf of the addict himself or of an appropriate third party, before a NARA III hearing can take place.

In *Gillespie*, however, after petitioning successfully for the NARA III commitment of an addict, the United States Attorney's Office proceeded without delay to obtain an indictment against the same individual. In ordering the indictment dismissed without prejudice, the court held, in effect, that: (1) the United States attorney is without discretion to refuse to file a NARA III petition on behalf of an addict otherwise qualified under the statute, and (2) that having filed a petition leading to adjudication and civil commitment, the United States attorney must observe the rule that the addict concerned "may not properly be indicted or tried so long as a civil NARA proceeding is pending."[16] In so holding, the court relied heavily on an analysis of the legislative history of NARA with its strong general emphasis on the desirability of noncriminal, nonstigmatic alternatives to prosecution of narcotics addicts. Although neither NARA nor its legislative history contained any express limitation on the exercise of independent discretion by the prosecutor, the court in *Gillespie* inferred restrictions on the prosecutor's discretionary powers and—as a necessary corollary—expansion of the discretionary powers of the court, which is charged by the statute with determining whether a particular addict should be committed under NARA III after a petition has been filed.

The conclusion of the court in *Gillespie*, if widely followed could have far-reaching implications for addict-diversion programs created by legislation that does not specifically provide for a prosecutorial veto. In addition, the holding of *Gillespie* might apply with equal force to addict-diversion programs created pursuant to judicial rule-making power. However, the reasoning of *Gillespie* depends on two unexamined but disputable propositions: (1) that prosecutorial discretion over the charging process can be legislatively or judicially divested, consistent with the separation of powers doctrine, and (2) that such a divestment may be accomplished by implication as well as by specific legislative directive.

The foregoing opinions recognize that under most circumstances the decision to charge is a valid function of the prosecutor. The process that leads to acquittal, dismissal of charges, and sentencing, or the exercise of sentencing discretion, is inherently a judicial function. Once formal charges are filed by way of arraignment, indictment, or information, determining the ultimate disposition of the case is primarily a judicial function, regardless of the advisory role assigned to the prosecutor by the court.[17]

The Decision to Terminate Unsuccessful Participation

It is likely that the agency having the power to place a person in a diversionary program would retain the power to terminate his participation. The prosecutor who has agreed to defer prosecution in a precharge-diversion program would have the responsibility to determine when prosecution should be resumed. This, of course, does not mean that he retains the same unreviewable discretion that he exercised in diverting in the first instance. The divertee, in order to participate in the program, does waive certain constitutional rights in reliance on the benefits of the program as presented to him by the prosecutor or program agents. Thus, how the power to terminate is exercised may involve a variety of legal problems; the existence of the power is likely to withstand legal challenge.[18]

In programs that divert after charges are filed, the courts would be an integral part of any termination decision. The formal charging process initiates the judicial process in which the court becomes the moving force and decision maker. This is evidenced by a variety of rules that demonstrate the discretion of the prosecutor diminishes upon formal charging. In many jurisdictions charges cannot by dismissed without court approval.[19] Guilty pleas cannot be withdrawn nor bail revoked except upon court order. Similarly, it would seem that termination of diversion granted after the judicial process is initiated would be a judicial function.

Notes

1. *See generally* ABA STANDARDS, PROSECUTING FUNCTION § 3.9 (1971). Of course the discretion is not unlimited. *See* Note, *The Right to Nondiscriminatory Enforcement of State Penal Laws,* 61 COLUM. L. REV. 1103 (1961). *See also* the discussion in Chapter 3, *supra.*

2. ABA Standards, *supra* note 1, at § 3.8.

3. Thompson v. State, 61 Wis.2d 325, 212 N.W.2d 109 (1973). The court held the discretion of the prosecuting attorney not reviewable in the courts regarding a prosecution/civil commitment choice.

4. *See,* however, United States v. Jacobsen, 16 CRIM. L. RPTR. 2005 (N.D. Tex. 1974) (court retains power to refuse to dismiss charges even if dismissal was promised by prosecution during plea negotiations).

5. 11 Cal.3d 59, 520 P.2d 405, 113 Cal. Rptr. 21 (1974).

6. 3 Cal.3d 89, 473 P.2d 993, 89 Cal. Rptr. 249 (1970).

7. *Id.* at 94, 473 P.2d at 996, 89 Cal. Rptr. at 252.

8. People v. Navarro, 7 Cal.3d 248, 497 P.2d 481, 102 Cal. Rptr. 137 (1972).

9. Esteybar v. Municipal Court, 5 Cal.3d 119, 485 P.2d 1140, 95 Cal. Rptr. 524 (1971).

10. People v. Clay, 18 Cal. App.3d 964, 96 Cal. Rptr. 213 (1971).

11. People v. Superior Court of San Mateo County, 11 Cal.3d 59, 66, 520 P.2d 405, 410, 113 Cal. Rptr. 21, 26 (1974).

12. *See* People v. Sanders, 522 P.2d 735 (Colo. 1974) (approving prosecutorial concurrence for release on recognizance).

13. 345 F. Supp. 1236 (W.D. Mo. 1972).

14. 42 U.S.C. § 3401 et seq. (1970).

15. 345 F. Supp. at 241–42.

16. *Id.* at 1238.

17. Some programs may also raise legal issues regarding the delegation of governmental powers. While the widespread use of administrative agencies has eroded the earlier doctrines prohibiting the delegation of governmental authority in regulatory matters, there remains substantial issues regarding delegation within the criminal justice system. *See* DAVIS ADMINISTRATIVE LAW § 2.14 (1970 Supp.). A rule retaining vitality prohibits the delegation to private parties of the power to establish penalties for criminal conduct. *Id.* at §2.13. Thus diversion programs granting veto power to private individuals, such as victims, would be suspect.

18. See Chapter 7, *infra.*

19. 21 AM.JUR. 2d. *Criminal Law* § 516 (1965).

6

Addiction-Treatment Records and Confidentiality

In the course of supervising and treating divertees referred from the criminal justice system, addiction therapy programs and their personnel will accumulate a range of sensitive information concerning these persons and their condition. Program records will detail each divertee's medical and psychiatric history, his exploratory test results, his diagnosis and prognosis, the prescriptions he receives, the courses of treatment recommended for him, the treatment he actually undergoes, and the observations of program personnel on his progress or lack thereof—the sorts of data conventionally assembled by a healer dealing with a patient's clinical problem. And because periodic urine testing is a special feature of most modes of addiction therapy, files of urinalysis results reflecting a divertee's drug-use patterns will be compiled. In addition, other program records will include especially sensitive personal data of the sort conventionally associated with psychiatric rather than clinical care: confidences disclosed by the divertee to his therapist or counsellor, which may reflect, among other things, details of his criminal career. Finally, addiction-therapy programs will develop a variety of essentially administrative records concerning their criminal justice patients, most notably those incorporating identification data—such as photographs—which are thought necessary to insure against abuse of program privileges by patients and nonpatients. Taken together, the written dossier, which a treatment program inevitably will compile concerning a divertee referred to its care, is a formidable one. Other data, not committed to paper, will nevertheless be revealed to and mentally noted by treatment staff; although the substance of such oral communications is less accessible in practice than the contents of a treatment file, they are potential subjects of inquiry.

By virtue of their special familiarity with their clients' histories, the personnel of addiction-treatment facilities accepting divertees from the criminal justice system can expect to receive a variety of requests and demands for information. Some will be of the sort familiar to all private physicians and public health organizations acting for drug abusers: inquiries from insurance companies and credit investigators, from patients' prospective employers, from agencies engaged in research, and even from parties to civil litigation in which a patient's condition is a disputed issue. Others will stem primarily from the addict–divertee's continuing status as

95

a criminal defendant or from his self-identification as a former participant in the criminal–addict subculture: inquiries from the courts as to active divertees' progress in treatment, from prosecutors or defense attorneys concerning the treatment records of former divertees now facing new or revived criminal charges, and from law enforcement agencies conducting general investigations of drug trafficking or other narcotics-related offenses. These inquiries will range in formality from casual contacts to administrative or judicial subpoenas. Each such inquiry, however, will pose a distinct challenge to the observance of the policy of confidentiality, which is presumed generally to be essential in maintaining a therapeutic relationship between the drug abuser and his physician or counsellor.

Before entering treatment as divertees, addicts may wish to know what assurance they can be given that the details of their treatment will remain confidential between themselves and the treatment facilities to which they are referred. Even if they do not request to know details they should be informed as a matter of routine, since expectations of confidentiality may figure in the choice between volunteering for diversion and submitting to conventional criminal processing. Some degree of confidentiality must be foregone by a divertee in order that he may conform to a program design. Almost inevitably, for example, addiction-therapy programs caring for divertees will be required to render progress reports to the courts. Insofar as positive guarantees of confidentiality cannot be afforded, the risks of disclosure should be elaborated before any defendant is asked to make an election between treatment and prosecution. Indeed, less than full disclosure may have constitutional ramifications since it detracts from the "intelligent" waiver of rights, inevitably required to participate in a diversion program.[1]

The extent of the confidentiality of information disclosed to diversion staff is determined in part by state and federal laws. The problem of confidentiality arises in two contexts. In the first, outside agencies seek to obtain information over the resistance of persons in whom confidence has been reposed such as where police seek information from treatment staff about persons participating in treatment. The issue here is the extent to which treatment staff may resist such requests. In the second, the patient seeks to prevent the disclosure of information where the treatment staff is willing to make it available to others. The legal issue here focuses on the patients' rights to confidentiality.

The Plea-bargain Cases

The addict-diversion program involves negotiations between the prosecutor and the accused that are similar to traditional plea bargaining. The

United States Supreme Court has suggested a constitutional requirement that prosecutorial agreements made in the course of plea bargains be kept.[2] Thus, the extent to which the records of the divertee are to be kept confidential can be agreed upon in advance and that agreement arguably would be enforced as a matter of constitutional law. There are of course a number of practical and legal difficulties with relying on this as a means of insuring the confidentiality of divertee's records.

First, in all likelihood the negotiations between the diversion staff and the accused will not result in any specific agreements on confidentiality nor will prosecutors be willing to grant complete confidentiality to information received during the diversion period. Indeed, the bargaining power of the accused in that situation does not provide leverage for insuring confidentiality.

Second, there may be a legal question regarding whether diversion staff are sufficiently a part of the prosecution to be bound by agreements or by the plea-bargaining cases. Where the diversion staff is part of an agency unrelated to the prosecution, an agreement by the prosecutor as part of a pretrial-diversion program may not bind others.

Third, the remedy available in the event of a breach of a plea bargain is not clear. The Supreme Court, while indicating a constitutional obligation on the part of the prosecution to abide by the bargain, refused to fashion a remedy.[3] The case involved prosecutorial promises regarding sentence recommendations. The Court remanded the case to the state courts to determine whether the circumstances required specific performance of the bargain or the withdrawal of the plea. Justice Douglas in concurrence, argued that the petitioner's desire regarding the remedy selected should be given great weight. In a bargain involving confidentiality of information, withdrawal of a guilty plea would not be an effective remedy. Indeed, the only remedy with meaning may be a prohibition against the use of wrongfully disclosed information adversely to the interests of the accused.

The Federal Statutes

The confidentiality of patient records in many addiction-therapy programs will be governed by the provisions of the Comprehensive Drug Abuse Prevention and Control Act of 1970,[4] and Section 408 of the Federal Drug Abuse Office and Treatment Act of 1972.[5] The federal legislation, however, has its own limitations. The 1970 act is restricted in coverage to "persons engaged in research," and creates mechanisms by which researchers can insure authorization to withhold the names and identifying characteristics of their subjects; it does not require that authorized researchers exercise this privilege of nondisclosure after it is granted to them. The 1972 act, by contrast, makes certain disclosures of addiction-treatment data a criminal offense, but it contains a mechanism by which the disclosure of records maintained by treatment programs within the act's coverage can be compelled by "a court of competent jurisdiction" after "application showing good cause therefor."[6]

The 1970 act gives both the secretary of HEW and the attorney general power to grant confidentiality to persons "engaged in research." The applicable provision reads:

The Attorney General may authorize persons engaged in research to withhold the names and other identifying characteristics of persons who are the subjects of such research. Persons who obtain this authorization may not be compelled in any Federal, State, or local civil, criminal, administrative, legislative, or other proceeding to identify the subjects of research for which such authorization was obtained.[7]

There are several obvious difficulties with relying on this statute as a basis for protecting the confidentiality of records of persons diverted to treatment programs. In the first instance, the program must be a "research" program. A program using experimental drugs or receiving federal financial backing to collect data on the progress of addicts committed to its care may qualify as a "research" effort.[8] By making application to the Departments of HEW or Justice, administrators can determine in advance whether they are entitled to assert an absolute privilege against the disclosure of certain information concerning their patients.

Second, the confidentiality provision applies only to patients' names and other identifying characteristics. Thus, once a person's identity is established by other means, the 1970 provision may not prohibit compelled disclosures relating to his subsequent treatment history.

Third, the provision does not prohibit treatment staff from voluntarily disclosing any information. While the staff would have a real interest in maintaining confidentiality of their voluntary patients in order to insure a continued base upon which to conduct research, persons transferred to their program under the pressure of a diversion policy may not be viewed with the same perspective. The pressures to disclose identifying information, particularly to law enforcement officials investigating serious criminal conduct, may temper the confidentiality granted by the 1970 act.

The Drug Abuse Office and Treatment Act of 1972, as amended, takes a substantially different approach to the problem of confidentiality of treatment records. Section 408 of the statute provides:

(a) Records of the identity, diagnosis, prognosis, or treatment of any patient which are maintained in connection with the performance of any drug abuse prevention function conducted, regulated, or directly or indirectly assisted by any department or agency of the United States shall, except as provided in subsection (e) of this section, be confidential and be disclosed only for the purposes and under the circumstances expressly authorized under subsection (b) of this section.

(b) (1) The content of any record referred to in subsection (a) of this section may be disclosed in accordance with the prior written consent of the patient with respect to whom such record is maintained, but only to such extent, under such circumstances, and for such purposes as may be allowed under regulations prescribed pursuant to subsection (g) of this section.

(2) Whether or not the patient, with respect to whom any given record referred to in subsection (a) of this section is maintained, gives his written consent, the content of such record may be disclosed as follows:

(A) To medical personnel to the extent necessary to meet a bona fide medical emergency.

(B) To qualified personnel for the purpose of conducting scientific research, management audits, financial audits, or program evaluation but such personnel may not identify, directly or indirectly, any individual patient in any report of such research, audit, or evaluation, or otherwise disclose patient identities in any manner.

(C) If authorized by an appropriate order of a court of competent jurisdiction granted after application showing good cause therefor. In assessing good cause the court shall weigh the public interest and the need for disclosure against the injury to the patient, to the physician-patient relationship, and to the treatment services. Upon the granting of such order, the court, in determining the extent to which any disclosure of all or any part of any record is necessary, shall impose appropriate safeguards against unauthorized disclosure.

(c) Except as authorized by a court order granted under subsection (b) (2)(C) of this section, no record referred to in subsection (a) of this section may be used to initiate or substantiate any criminal charges against a patient or to conduct any investigation of a patient.

(d) The prohibitions of this section continue to apply to records concerning any individual who has been a patient, irrespective of whether or when he ceases to be a patient.

(e) The prohibitions of this section do not apply to any interchange of records—

(1) within the Armed Forces or within those components of the Veterans' Administration furnishing health care to veterans, or

(2) between such components and the Armed Forces.

(f) Any person who violates any provision of this section or any regulation issued pursuant to this section shall be fined not more than $500 in the case of a first offense, and not more than $5,000 in the case of each subsequent offense.

(g) The Secretary of Health, Education, and Welfare, after consultation with the Administrator of Veterans' Affairs and the heads of other Federal departments and agencies substantially affected thereby, shall prescribe regulations to carry out the purposes of this section. These regulations may contain such definitions, and may provide for such safeguards and procedures, including procedures and criteria for the issuance and scope of orders under subsection (b) (2) (C) of this section, as in the judgment of the Secretary are necessary or proper to effectuate the purposes of this section, to prevent circumvention or evasion thereof, or to facilitate compliance therewith.[9]

The 1972 act, applicable to all federally assisted programs, does restrict the disclosure of treatment information without a patient's express consent. However, questions arise as to how seriously the principle of confidentiality is compromised by subsection (b) (2) (C) permitting disclosure without the patient's consent pursuant to court order.

The current regulations promulgated by the secretary of Health, Education, and Welfare under subsection (g) of the statute have not only widely extended the applicability of the confidentiality provisions but have given some content to and limitation on the power of courts to order disclosure of patient records.[10] While earlier regulations issuing out of the Special Action Office were generally phrased and more cautious in interpreting the language of the statute, the present regulations recognize at the outset the tension between the public interest and that of a participant in drug-abuse programs. The stated purpose of the regulations is to

implement the authorizing legislation in a manner that, to the extent practicable, takes into account two streams of legal thought and social policy. One has to do with enhancing the quality and attractiveness of treatment systems. The other is concerned with the interests of patients as citizens, most particularly in regard to protecting their rights of privacy. Within each stream there are crosscurrents, and it should come as no surprise that areas of turbulence are to be found at their confluence.[11]

The interpretative regulations greatly expand the programs subject to the act and the confidentiality regulations. The statutory language applies to any program "directly or indirectly assisted by any department or agency of the United States." While earlier regulations had given this a restricted interpretation, the current regulations include within the "indirectly assisted" language any program that uses federal funds including general revenue sharing funds or is "assisted by the Internal Revenue Service . . . through the allowance of income tax deductions for contributions to the program. . . ."[12] It would appear that only privately operated profit-oriented drug-abuse programs would not be governed by the statute and accompanying regulations although the intent of Congress to apply the act solely on the basis of the hidden subsidies in the Internal Revenue Code is far from clear.

Perhaps the most critical limitation in the regulations on the power of courts to order disclosure provides that the court cannot require disclosure of "communications by a patient to personnel of the program. . . ."[13] Only such information as "facts or dates of enrollment, discharge, attendance, medication, and similar objective data" can be disclosed by court order.[14] The apparent thrust of the regulations is to make the scope of the confidentiality provided by the statute coextensive with what is traditionally protected by the doctor–patient privilege. The regulations in fact appear to extend the privilege to all personnel of the program whether or not they are medically trained.

The regulations are not, however, free from ambiguity of potential legal significance. It is not, for example, altogether clear that the exemption of "communications" from disclosure by court order is authorized by the act. The authority of the secretary to promulgate regulations is conferred by subsection (g) of the statute and permits definitions, safeguards, procedures, and criteria "for the issuance and scope of orders." However, such regulations must either (1) effectuate the purposes of the section; (2) prevent circumvention or evasion of the section; or (3) facilitate compliance therewith. It is not clear that the exemption for communications fits either of the purposes for which the secretary is authorized to act; rather it may serve to limit the section's purpose beyond that desired by Congress. Congress was clearly unwilling to enact a complete privilege for drug-abuse programs nor was it willing to exempt from disclosure information that might injure the "physician–patient relationship." Congress was willing to provide for confidentiality subject to review by a court and subject to disclosure when the court determined it was in the public interest. The exemption of "communications" may be construed to offend rather than effectuate that purpose.

The line between communications and objective data is not always a bright one. Much objective data in a patient's file may have been obtained from the "communications" of patients. And even hard data showing admittance to a drug-abuse treatment program or the pursuit of certain treatment modalities may still have an adverse affect on the life of the divertee. While the current regulations move a long way toward removing impediments to entry into diversion programs, it should be recognized that there still remains a substantial risk of collateral consequences to a decision to seek diversion.

Section 2.64 of the regulations specifies in some detail requisite procedures for disclosure pursuant to "court orders" including prior notice to patients and administrators and hearings conducted (absent a patient's request for an open hearing) in judge's chambers, as well as restating the generally phrased balancing considerations (e.g., "adverse effects" on treatment of patient or program operations, against "need for privacy").[15] The regulation also provides in some new detail the necessary elements of an order granting disclosure, including an express direction that all such orders shall state limitations on what is to be disclosed and to whom. Section 2.65 directs that no order issue except where the program maintaining the records has been adequately represented by counsel independent of counsel for the moving party or applicant; it does not prescribe a general rule that the interests of an affected patient, as distinct from those of the program in which he is enrolled, be represented through independent counsel.[16]

The regulations speak directly to the disclosure of records by court order for the purpose of conducting an investigation or prosecution of a patient—perhaps the most sensitive area of conflict between public and private interest. Section 2.65 provides in part:

(c) Criteria. A court may authorize disclosure of records pertaining to a patient for the purpose of conducting an investigation of or a prosecution for a crime of which the patient is suspected only if the court finds that all of the following criteria are met:

(1) The crime was extremely serious, such as one involving kidnapping, homicide, assault with a deadly weapon, armed robbery, rape, or other acts causing or directly threatening loss of life or serious bodily injury, or was believed to have been committed on the premises of the program or against personnel of the program.

(2) There is a reasonable likelihood that the records in question will disclose material information or evidence of substantial value in connection with the investigation or prosecution.

(3) There is no other practicable way of obtaining the information or evidence.

(4) The actual or potential injury to the physician–patient relationship in the program affected and in other programs similarly situated, and the actual or potential harm to the ability of such programs to attract and retain patients, is outweighed by the public interest in authorizing the disclosure sought.

(d) Scope. Both disclosure and dissemination of any information from the records in question shall be limited under the terms of the order to assure that no information will be unnecessarily disclosed and that dissemination will be no wider than necessary. Under no circumstances may an order under this section authorize a program to turn over patient records in general, pursuant to a subpoena or otherwise, to a grand jury or a law enforcement, investigative, or prosecutorial agency.[17]

Although this language represents substantial progress toward clarity, it leaves unresolved such critical questions as the interpretation of "acts . . . directly threatening . . . serious bodily injury." Would, for example, this include an allegation that a patient has been engaging in small narcotics sale transactions? If not, would sale transactions of a wholesale nature be "acts" of the type contemplated. All that can be safely said is that the language of the new regulations would appear to bar disclosure to investigators or prosecutors in cases of petty property crimes not involving any use, or threat of use, of physical force. In addition, it may be doubted that state courts will consistently abide by a federal "interpretative order" that purports to limit what may constitute the basis for a judicial determination of "good cause" in a state proceeding.

It should also be noted that the new regulations relating to "court orders" fail to prescribe specific rules for situations in which information concerning patients is sought for possible adverse use in "noncriminal" proceedings. A literal reading of the regulations and the act suggest that in these circumstances the records can be sought from the treatment program and disclosed by the court regardless of the nature of the proposed use and without any required participation by the patient.

Finally the new regulations should be seen as providing a salutary reminder that the provisions of the statute may be subject to waiver by persons seeking to enter treatment including prospective divertees. Section 2.39 specifically regulates the disclosure of information on patients referred to drug-abuse treatment programs by criminal justice agencies.[18] Section 2.39 provides:

(a) *Consent authorized.* Where participation by an individual in a treatment program is made a condition of such individual's release from confinement, the disposition or status of any criminal proceedings against him or the execution or suspension of any sentence imposed upon him, such individual may consent to unrestricted communication between any program in which he is enrolled in fulfillment of such condition and (1) the court granting probation, or other post-trial or pretrial conditional release, (2) the parole board or other authority granting parole, or (3) probation or parole officers responsible for his supervision.

(b) *Duration of consent.* Where consent is given for disclosures described in paragraph (a) of this section, such consent shall expire sixty days after it is given or when there is a substantial change in such person's status, whichever is later. For the purposes of this section, a substantial change occurs in the status of a person who, at the time such consent is given, has been—

(1) Arrested, when such person is formally charged or unconditionally released from arrest;

(2) Formally charged, when the charges have been dismissed with prejudice, or the trial of such person has been commenced;

(3) Brought to a trial which has commenced, when such person has been acquitted or sentenced;

(4) Sentenced, when the sentence has been fully executed.

(c) *Revocation of consent.* An individual whose release from confinement, probation, or parole is conditioned upon his participation in a treatment program may not revoke a consent given by him in accordance with paragraph (a) of this section until there has been a formal and effective termination or revocation of such release from confinement, probation, or parole.

(d) *Restrictions on redisclosure.* Any information directly or indirectly received pursuant to this section may be used by the recipients thereof only in connection with their official duties with respect to the particular individual with respect to whom it was acquired. Such recipients may not make such information available for general investigative purposes, or otherwise use it in unrelated proceedings or make it available for unrelated purposes.

The only reported court decisions involving the 1972 act, the opinions of the New York Supreme Court and Court of Appeals in the recent case of *People* v. *Newman*, [19] illustrate the difficulties inherent in its interpretation. The *Newman* case did not touch directly on the records of addict–divertees, but the various approaches taken by the courts suggest that a case involving divertee records might pose serious analytical problems. Like many demands for divertee-program records, the demand at issue in *Newman* was predicated on the public interest in efficient law enforcement. Following a fatal shooting, one witness tentatively identified the killer as a patient enrolled in a particular methadone-maintenance clinic. After the failure of informal police efforts to secure the cooperation of the New York City methadone-treatment administration in gaining a positive identification, a subpoena was sought and obtained directing the administrator, Dr. Robert Newman, to produce photographs of all Negro men between the ages of 21 and 35 who had been treated at the clinic in question in the 6 months preceding the shooting. Dr. Newman refused and was held in civil contempt. On a first appeal the contempt citation was vacated by a panel of the Appellate Division of the Supreme Court, which reasoned that although the subpoena in question was a court order within the meaning of Section 408 (b) (2) (C) of the 1972 federal act, it had been drafted more broadly than was necessary to accomplish the identification sought. The court redrew the terms of the subpoena to provide additional protection for the anonymity of patients whose photographs would not be singled out by the police witness. Dr. Newman still refused to comply.

On the appeal that followed the Court of Appeals struck down the subpoena—but not because it was a court order of a sort outside the statutory exception to the confidentiality provisions of the 1972 act. Instead, the Court of Appeals concluded that Dr. Newman's particular methadone-treatment program was authorized to assert an absolute privilege against the disclosure of identifying data under the terms of the *1970* federal act. The court rejected the argument that the more flexible provisions of the 1972 act had repealed by implication the mandatory confidentiality provisions of the 1970 statute that Dr. Newman asserted. The court based its view in substantial part on the fact that the agencies involved had interpreted the statutes as not being in conflict.

The final result in the *Newman* case does not amount to a declaration that the 1972 act generally bars court orders to secure addiction-treatment records for use in criminal proceedings. On the contrary, it suggests that there are many drug-treatment programs, falling outside the coverage of the 1970 act, which could be forced to comply with such orders. Only the special status of the New York City methadone program as an "important drug-addiction research" effort, whose participants had been specifically granted "unconditional" anonymity by the secretary of Health, Education and Welfare and the attorney general, saved Dr. Newman the hard choice between disclosure and punishment for contempt.[20] Nor is it clear that even the limited holding of *Newman* would be followed in other jurisdictions. In a strongly reasoned dissent, Judge Breitel of the Court of Appeals concluded that the absolute confidentiality provisions of the 1970 act should be read as having been repealed by implication through the

Congress' adoption of the conditional confidentiality provisions of the 1972 act, and that all addiction-treatment records afforded any protection under federal law should be considered subject to compelled disclosure upon issuance of an appropriate court order. Judge Breitel's position is one that other courts considering the scope of federal confidentiality legislation reasonably could adopt.

State Drug-abuse Treatment Confidentiality Statutes

In addition to the federal acts of 1970 and 1972, there exist a number of state laws specifically designed to give drug-abuse treatment programs and patients a measure of privilege against compelled disclosure of sensitive information. Although these drug-abuse treatment statutes are of relatively recent vintage, and have been little construed, they can nonetheless be classified into three groups. The first, comprising the New Mexico,[21] Georgia,[22] and Oklahoma[23] statutes, consist of serious attempts to legislate a balance of the interests of confidentiality and disclosure. The New Mexico scheme seems to provide a substantial measure of confidentiality. The Georgia and Oklahoma attempts are only partially effective. Both, for example, apply only to patients enrolled in state-sanctioned programs but not to those participating in unsupported programs, while the Georgia statute is ambiguous as to what information is privileged, and neither statute provides any penalty for violations by treatment staff.

A second group consists of statutes with serious defects as bulkheads against disclosure of sensitive information accumulated by "addict-diversion" programs. The Hawaii,[24] Kansas,[25] and Nebraska[26] statutes, for example, have the effect of diluting those states' general physician–patient privilege statutes where alcoholism or drug-abuse treatment patients are concerned, while the relatively inclusive Missouri laws extend no privilege to a patient against whom criminal charges are pending.[27] The New Hampshire statute applies only to minors.[28]

Finally there exist a third group of state drug-abuse treatment confidentiality statutes, which are either so limited in their terms,[29] or so uncertain in their coverage,[30] that their significance, if any, for the organization of "addict-diversion" programs cannot be accurately gauged; because of their peculiar character, no planner or prospective participant should rely heavily on the protection they appear to afford until they are the subject of clarification.

Consideration of any privilege or confidentiality statute, specifically applicable to information collected or disclosed during drug-abuse treatment is of obvious importance to any analysis of the degree of real

security that a participant's privacy will be afforded after his or her enrollment in addict diversion.

A recently amended provision of the California diversion statute
reflects the obvious tensions between the needs of the criminal justice
system and the privacy interests of individuals considered for or enrolled
in diversion programs. The California statute related to confidentiality of
treatment records reads:

No statement, or any information procured therefrom, made by the defendant to
any probation officer or drug treatment worker, which is made during the course
of any investigation conducted by the probation department or drug treatment
program pursuant to subdivision (b), and prior to the reporting of the probation
department's findings and recommendations to the court, shall be admissible in
any action or proceeding brought subsequent to the investigation.

No statement, or any information procured therefrom, with respect to the
specific offense with which the defendant is charged, which is made to any probation officer or drug program worker subsequent to the granting of diversion, shall
be admissible in any action or proceeding.

In the event that diversion is either denied, or is subsequently revoked once
it has been granted, neither the probation investigation nor statements or information divulged during that investigation shall be used in any sentencing procedures.[31]

While the statute seeks to provide a strong measure of confidentiality
to information disclosed to diversion program personnel, the limitations
in the statute and the failure to provide for a prohibition against derivative
use of disclosed statements and information still force the defendant to a
hard choice in fully revealing his past drug history.

General State Treatment Privilege Statutes

The legal status of information about addict–divertees under the applicable state laws will vary among jurisdictions and treatment programs. In
states that have created a testimonial physician–patient (or psychologist–client) privilege by statute, the statute's particular terms will bar
compelled disclosure of certain sorts of information by certain addiction-
treatment personnel in certain proceedings. The limitations on and exceptions to a statute's coverage may permit other forms of disclosure to be
compelled. Since no physician–patient privilege existed at common law,
the laws of those states that have not enacted privilege statutes leave all
information gathered in therapeutic relationships potentially subject to
compulsory disclosure. And even where the most comprehensive state
statutes creating a privilege are in force, they amount to mere rules of evidence, which a patient may invoke in judicial or quasi-judicial proceedings, and which a healer is obliged to invoke on his patient's behalf.[32]

A discussion of some hypothetical examples may illustrate the wide range of problems that confront diversion staff in their efforts to determine what guarantees of confidentiality they can offer to prospective program participants.

The simplest case is that of an independent, privately financed, "drug-free" treatment program operating in a state with no privilege statute conferring confidential status on information developed in physician–patient or psychologist–client relationships. It is assumed the federal confidentiality legislation would not reach out to cover a treatment effort of this design. Consequently, the personnel of this treatment program would be without legal justification in resisting a subpoena for records or testimony concerning their patients, whether issued in the course of civil litigation, a criminal prosecution, a legislative hearing, or a grand jury investigation. In addition, they could be compelled to make reports on their patients to a state health commission or board, if such reporting were required by statute.[33] Under these circumstances, a potential addict–divertee should be informed not only that regular evaluative reports on his progress in treatment *will* be transmitted to the court from which he was diverted, but also that the raw data contained in his file and the recollections of treatment staff concerning his case *may* be put to a wide variety of nontherapeutic—and potentially damaging—uses. And since a right of confidentiality does not exist here, no express waiver need be secured from a potential divertee before such information regarding him may be disclosed.[34]

The status of the records of an identical treatment facility operating in a state with medical confidentiality legislation is more difficult to analyze, because state privilege statutes, as written and interpreted, are hedged with multiple exceptions. Although, as a general matter, treatment history of an addict–divertee will be entitled to the same protection from compelled disclosure as that of a free, self-referred patient entering the same therapeutic program,[35] this protection is by no means complete. Its extent will depend, among other things, on the purposes for which disclosure is sought, the identity of the treatment staff member to whom it was first made known, and the exact nature of the data in question.

First, it should be noted that certain state statutes apply only in civil proceedings.[36] Such an exception dictates the peculiar result that while an addict–divertee's records would be unavailable in a divorce proceeding brought by his or her spouse, they could be compelled for use against the patient if prosecution were resumed on the very charge that initially led to his diversion; since the course of addiction therapy may include admissions of past drug use and criminal conduct made to treatment personnel, the defense of a formerly diverted addict–defendant could be severely disadvantaged by an unsuccessful attempt at pretrial treatment.

The exclusion of criminal cases is the most common of those exceptions to the statutory physician–patient privilege that relate to the intended use of the data sought. As a general matter, it can be said that where the privilege exists it can be asserted in technically nonjudicial, as well as judicial, proceedings. If a doctor's testimony or records are not available at a criminal trial, they are also beyond the reach of a grand jury subpoena;[37] if an order for the production of medical records is outside the competence of a court of law, a legislative committee has no greater authority.[38] Thus, whether disclosure of an addict–divertee's treatment history can be compelled during a formal precharge investigation will usually turn on whether similar information could be ordered produced for use as trial evidence.

Second, it should be emphasized that even in states that extend a physician–patient privilege to both criminal and civil proceedings, it is often unclear whether the privilege is applicable when information initially has been received by persons other than duly qualified physicians, working under physicians' general supervision. This circumstance will occur in drug-abuse therapy programs of all descriptions. One commentator recently has observed that "[I]n Wisconsin it is unclear whether the privilege applies to communications made to or in the presence of auxiliary medical personnel, such as nurses, medical students and technicians."[39] With specific reference to nurses, the nonphysician medical personnel whose participation is most essential in medical care delivery, another commentator has noted generally that "Most of the courts take the view that, even [where the nurse attending the patient acts as one of the necessary assistants or agents of the attending physician] the privilege does not apply...."[40] Thus, the testimony of nurses, and the production of medical records prepared exclusively by nurses, generally can be compelled. Even in the few jurisdictions that have moved to correct this apparent anomaly by bringing the limited class "licensed" or "trained" nurses within the express coverage of medical privilege statutes,[41] the confidential status of addiction-treatment records remains open to serious question, since most drug-therapy programs rely heavily on paramedical workers, ex-addict counsellors, and other nonlicensed personnel. Indeed, some "drug-free" treatment programs that may receive addict–divertees are not even generally supervised by licensed medical professionals; they are managed instead by "street-wise" ex-addicts, whose lack of formal credentials leaves them—and their assistants—altogether outside the coverage of privilege statutes.[42] And the general exclusion of nonprofessional treatment personnel from the coverage of state privilege statutes may have another important consequence for drug-abuse treatment programs. It may be impossible to resist legally a demand for the disclosure of urinalysis or other test results. Since these records are prepared exclusively by laboratory technicians, they may be subject to compelled disclosure even if they later are used by a physician or other treatment professional in assessing an addict–patient's condition.[43]

Third, even where a state statutory privilege applies to a proceeding in which information concerning a patient is sought, and where the persons who have the information are within the coverage of the statute, the privilege can be invoked only with respect to information of certain sorts. In a few jurisdictions, only data relating to the diagnosis and treatment of particular diseases or conditions is protected.[44] More generally, it is held that protection extends only to information that is "necessary" to the therapeutic process and that could not have been observed casually by a layman. One commentator has reviewed the case law and concluded that:

A physician is free to testify as to the fact of his employment by, or that he treated, the patient, the fact that the patient was sick, the place and duration of the treatment, and the date and numbers of his visits. The physician also may testify to the dates of the patient's entry into and his departure from a hospital, that he made an examination of the patient, that a diagnosis was made, that he recommended the taking of x-ray photographs, that he performed an operation on the patient, and he may state whether or not he discharged the patient as being well.... [T]he names and addresses of a physician's patients or those of a hospital are not privileged.[45]

In sum, a whole range of data concerning patients and their treatment, which might be characterized as "administrative" rather than medical in character, is outside the coverage of even the most inclusive state-privilege statutes. Where most physical ailments are concerned, this considerable gap in statutory coverage is probably of little significance, since the patient's main interest will be in preventing disclosure of the nature of his illness and of the treatment he has undergone. But to the addict or drug abuser, the very fact that he has entered treatment, along with his name or other identifying characteristics, may be matters that he strongly desires to remain confidential. A record of the number or frequency of his visits to a clinic may be almost as sensitive as the record of his progress in treatment.

Although it can be argued that to an addict–divertee anonymity necessarily is less critical than it may be to a free, self-referred addict–patient, it is nevertheless true that the terms of an individual's diversion plan will be known to relatively few persons or agencies; thus, the divertee retains a substantial interest in preventing the "administrative" details of his treatment from becoming more generally known. He may wish, for example, to prevent the disclosure of this information to the investigative arms of law enforcement agencies that were not concerned in his most recent contacts with the criminal justice system. Having entered treatment, he may wish in particular that information showing how long he remained in active care be kept from disclosure. Yet this is precisely the sort of data as to which addiction-treatment programs operating only under a state physician–patient privilege statute may be unable to guarantee full confidentiality. Prospective divertees should be notified in advance whether, under locally applicable statutes, the administrative details of their therapy will be subject to compelled disclosure.

The Patient's Right to Assert the Privilege

In many states the privilege statute restricting access to a patient's records does not expressly provide protection for the patient in the event his physician is willing to make the disclosure. However, in a number of cases courts have found a cause of action on behalf of patients for damages resulting from unauthorized disclosure.[46] Some cases have recognized that disclosure is a violation of the patient's right of privacy[47] while others have provided tort liability on the basis of a violation of a confidential relationship.[48] At least one case has indicated that the statutory physician–patient privilege creates a private cause of action on the patient's behalf.[49] It is thus possible that diversion staff face personal financial liability for unauthorized disclosure.

The common law doctrines used to support a patient's cause of action are not without defenses. Some courts have indicated that where disclosure is justified by an overriding public interest, the disclosure can be made by the physician without fear of liability to the patient. Thus treatment information has been disclosed justifiably to stop the spread of contagious disease[50] or to prevent fraud on an employer or an insurance company.[51] The scope of the public interest defense remains undefined, and many courts may be reluctant to find liability for disclosure of privileged information to law enforcement officers for any purpose.

Conclusion

The confidentiality of the treatment records of addict–divertees is a critical factor in assessing the value of diversion. The person offered diversion must make some very difficult choices. He is asked in many programs to waive substantial constitutional protections. He submits himself to what may appear to him to be intrusive therapy. His major incentive for participation may well be the hope of release without the stigma of a criminal conviction. Yet, the stigma of participation in addict therapy may be equally damaging to his long-term readjustment.

As the discussion above indicates, the extent to which his participation is in fact confidential remains a product of many factors, some of which are outside the power of the diversion staff to influence. Nowhere does there appear to be a provision that offers complete confidentiality in these programs. As one author noted: "If the decision whether to provide a privilege is to be made by balancing the needs of law-enforcement and rehabilitation approaches to drug abuse . . . the need for a rehabilitation approach seems to weigh more heavily."[52] At least until such legislation is enacted, organizers of addict-diversion programs must proceed cautiously in informing prospective divertees of the uses to which their treatment records may eventually be put.

Notes

1. Miranda v. Arizona, 384 U.S. 436 (1966), recognizes the "intelligent" aspect of a voluntary waiver regarding Fifth and Sixth Amendment protections. *See also* Barker v. Wingo, 407 U.S. 514 (1972), regarding the knowing waiver of the right to a speedy trial.

2. Santobello v. New York, 404 U.S. 257 (1971).

3. *Id.*

4. 42 U.S.C. § 242(a) (1970), 21 U.S.C. § 872(c) (1970).

5. 21 U.S.C. § 1175 (1972).

6. 21 U.S.C. § 1175 (b) (2) (C), as amended (1974).

7. 21 U.S.C. § 872(c) (1970). See also, 42 U.S.C. § 242 (a) (1970).

8. The category of treatment programs that, on application, can expect to receive formal authorization to maintain the form of absolute confidentiality contemplated in the 1970 act apparently now includes all programs dispensing methadone for maintenance purposes. The FDA's regulations for the administration of methadone programs expressly provide that: "[I]nformation that would identify the patient will be kept confidential . . . and will not be divulged in any civil, criminal, administrative or other proceedings. . . ." 37 Fed. Reg. 6943 (April 6, 1972).

9. 21 U.S.C. § 1175 (1972) as amended (1974).

10. Confidentiality of Alcohol and Drug Abuse Patient Records Regulations, 40 Fed. Reg. 27802 (1975).

11. Reg. § 2.4, 40 Fed. Reg. 27804 (1975).

12. Reg. § 2.12, *id.* at 27806.

13. Reg. § 2.63, *id.* at 27819.

14. *Id.*

15. *Id.* at 27820.

16. *Id.*

17. *Id.*

18. *Id.* at 27813–14.

19. 40 A.D.2d 633, N.Y.S.2d 127 (Sup. Ct. 1973), *rev'd,* 32 N.Y.2d 379, 298 N.E.2d 651, 345 N.Y.S.2d 502 (1973).

20. The quoted language was employed in a brief supporting Dr.

Newman's position filed with the Court of Appeals by the Special Action Office for Drug Abuse Prevention. *See* 345 N.Y.S.2d at 508.

21. NEW MEX. STAT. § 54-10-12, § 54-10-13 (Supp. 1973).

22. GA. CODE ANN. § 84-6318 (Supp. 1974). The provision prohibits the disclosure of the name of a drug-dependent person "who seeks or obtains treatment" and provides a privilege for "any communication" by such person to a member of the program staff. It is not clear that medical records other than those communicated to the staff by the patient are protected.

23. OKLA. STAT. ANN. tit. 43A § 657 (1971).

24. HAWAII REV. STAT. § 334-5 (Supp. 1973). The statute authorizes disclosure when a court believes it to be in the public interest.

25. KAN. STAT. ANN. § 65-4050 (1972) (applicable to alcoholism treatment). See also KAN. STAT. ANN. § 65-4134 (1972) providing an absolute privilege for the identity of a patient.

26. NEB. REV. STAT. § 83-163 (Reissue 1971).

27. MO. ANN. STAT. § 195.545 (1973).

28. N. H. REV. STAT. ANN. § 318-B:12-a (Supp. 1973).

29. TENN. CODE ANN. § 33-813 (Supp. 1974) (providing a variety of exceptions to confidentiality including court orders for good cause.

30. TEX. CODE CRIM. PROC. § 38.101 (Supp. 1974) (applicable only to voluntary patients).

31. CAL. PENAL CODE § 1000.1 (1976).

32. Other, more limited, statutes afford the patient only a right of objection, which is waived if not exercised. Under such statutes a physician may volunteer privileged testimony and may give it if his patient does not protest. *See, e.g.,* ANN. CODE MISS. § 13-1-21 (1972); and Gulf, Mobile & Ohio R. Co. v. Smith, 50 So. 2d 898, 901 (Miss. 1951).

33. *See* Felber v. Foote, 321 F. Supp. 85 (D. Conn. 1970), upholding the constitutionality of a Connecticut statute mandating reporting of the names and characteristics of "drug-dependent persons." Connecticut has no general physician–patient privilege statute, and its special phychiatrist–patient statute was deemed by the court not to invalidate the challenged reporting requirement.

34. To the extent that addiction-treatment programs view the requirement of regular reporting to a diverting court as being in potential conflict with their ethical duty to observe confidentiality, they may wish to request that divertees execute an express limited waiver covering this procedure before accepting those divertees as patients.

35. The special legal conditions attaching to a divertee's participation in treatment should not, in themselves, diminish the confidentiality of his

records. It is generally held, for example, that involuntary patients in public institutions have the privilege against the disclosure of their records as do voluntary fee-paying patients. *See, e.g.* Taylor v. United States, 222 F.2d 398 (D.C. Cir. 1955), *but see, contra,* State v. Murphy, 205 Iowa 1130, 217 N.W. 225 (1928).

36. *See, e.g.,* IDAHO CODE § 9-203 (Supp. 1974). In some other states the privilege extends to criminal actions but not those involving, for example, charges of rape, murder, and abortion.

37. *See* People v. Sellick, 4 N.Y. Crim. Rep. 329 (1886).

38. *See,* New York City Council v. Goldwater, 284 N.Y. 296, 31 N.E.2d 31 (1940).

39. Whiteford, *The Physician, the Law, and the Drug Abuser,* 119 U. PA. L. REV. 933, 958-59 (1971).

40. C. DEWITT, PRIVILEGED COMMUNICATIONS BETWEEN PHYSICIAN AND PATIENT 92 (1958).

41. *See, e.g.,* ARK. STAT. ANN. § 28-607 (1962).

42. In recognition of the fact that sensitive disclosures are an essential element of forms of therapy to which the principle of physician–patient confidentiality has not previously been uniformly extended, a number of states have recently enacted special legislation creating a new confidential privilege in the field of psychotherapy. Some of these new statutes protect only disclosures made to licensed M.D.'s practicing psychotherapy (*see, e.g.,* CONN. GEN. STAT. § 52-146 [1974]), while others cover trained psychologists as well (*see, e.g.,* ALASKA STAT. § 90, 86.200 [1973]), and a few even take in disclosures made to certain social workers (*see, e.g.,* CAL. EVIDENCE CODE § 1010c [1973 Suppl]). Frequently, they provide more protection than is afforded to the confidences divulged in a conventional physician–patient relationship. In Connecticut, for example, there is a statutory privilege covering the records of mental patients, but none for the records of medical patients in general; in California, the general patient–physician privilege is wholly inapplicable in criminal proceedings, while disclosures made to psychiatrists and licensed psychologists are protected from disclosure in most prosecutions.

The movement toward statutory recognition of the confidential nature of communications made during psychotherapy may have some impact on the confidentiality of addiction treatment records—where such treatment is conducted by a "psychotherapist" within the meaning of one of the new statutes. But this impact will be limited, since the new statutes, like the more familiar legislation governing compelled disclosure of medical confidences in general, protect only information made known to qualified professionals, and generally only that made known to state-licensed professionals. Although an ex-addict paraprofessional drug-abuse counsellor may be practicing a form of psychotherapy in fact, his testimony and his records will receive no additional protection from compelled discovery in a state that has enacted a psychotherapist's privilege statute.

43. For the analogous view that where technicians are outside the coverage of a privilege statute, hospital x-rays are not privileged, *see* Leusink v. O'Donnell, 255 Wisc. 627, 39 N.W.2d 675 (1949).

44. *See, e.g.,* PA. STAT. ANN. tit. 28 § 328 (1958) (limiting the privilege to "information . . . which shall tend to blacken the character of the patient. . . .") In People v. Newman, *supra* note 12, the Court of Appeals held the state privilege statute inapplicable to photographs of a patient since these records were "obtained by the appellant's staff during administrative admission procedures . . . not to enable the doctor to act in his 'professional capacity' but to prevent unregistered patients from receiving methadone and registered patients from receiving the wrong dosage. . . ." 345 N.Y.S.2d at 505.

45. DEWITT, *supra* note 32, at 146–149.

46. *See generally* Annot., Physician's Tort Liability, Apart From Defamation, for Unauthorized Disclosure of Confidential Information About Patients, 20 A.L.R.3d 1109 (1968).

47. Hammonds v. Aetna Casualty & Surety Co., 243 F. Supp. 793 (N.D. Ohio 1965).

48. Felis v. Greenberg, 51 Misc.2d 441, 273 N.Y.S.2d 288 (Sup. Ct. 1966).

49. Simonsen v. Swenson, 104 Neb. 224, 177 N.W. 831 (1920).

50. *Id.*

51. Clark v. Geraci, 29 Misc.2d 791, 208 N.Y.S.2d 564 (1960).

52. Whitford, *supra* note 31, at 959.

7

Termination of Diversion

Not every addict–defendant diverted to treatment will succeed in showing progress toward ending dependence on illicit drugs. Among those who do not, there will be "failures" of different kinds: some will have been unable to reduce illicit drug use even though they have made good faith attempts to comply with a therapeutic regimen; others will have records that reflect continuing drug use and sporadic cooperation in prescribed treatment routines; and still others will have made no effort whatsoever to realize for themselves benefits potentially available through treatment. In addition to these "treatment failures," there will be other divertees against whom it may be necessary to consider resuming prosecution: the "administrative failures" who will have proved so disruptive that their continued presence cannot be tolerated by the treatment program to which they have been referred, and those who have been charged with new criminal offenses while on diversionary status. Termination of diversion is a serious step by definition, and the practical problem of insuring fairness at termination can be expected to become increasingly acute.

The legal issues involved in such a termination are substantial. This chapter will consider three basic ones: (1) what are legally permissible grounds for termination; (2) what procedures are required in terminating a person's diversion program; and (3) what legally permissible results can follow from termination?

Grounds for Termination

Two separate lines of authority support a constitutional requirement that a divertee must be found to have violated one of the conditions of his diversion before that program can be terminated. The diversion of an accused, particularly in a program requiring a conditional plea of guilty, is a result of bargaining in which the accused has a substantial interest in having the authorities live up to their side of the bargain. In addition, cases involving parole and probation revocation suggest that due process may require that once a person is diverted he has a right to continue in that program until he is shown to have violated one of the conditions of his entry.

115

The Plea-bargain Cases

The person participating in a diversion program is forced to waive several constitutional rights. This waiver is based on the opportunity for drug treatment on conditions generally stated to the person in advance. Recently the United States Supreme Court has underscored the legal rule that prosecuting authorities should live up to agreements made during plea negotiations.[1] Taking this case as an analogy, a divertee could not be terminated from a diversion program unless he violated a condition of his diversion.

A difficult question may arise in defining what the basis of the bargain between the addict and the program staff is. Does he have to continue in treatment programs or does he have to be successfully "cured"? Is arrest for another offense a violation? Is evidence of further drug use sufficient to terminate? The legal problem facing diversion staff is that if the conditions for continued participation are not stipulated in advance, the courts will be forced to interpret what was intended.[2] It would be wise practice to provide each person diverted with a written list of the factors that would justify his termination.

The Parole- and Probation-revocation Cases

In recent years, the United States Supreme Court has recognized that due process requires certain protections when the state seeks to "revoke" a person on probation or parole. In imposing these requirements, the Court has assumed that a factual question inevitably exists as to whether the person did or did not violate the conditions imposed upon him. In *Morrissey* v. *Brewer* the Court expressly recognized that "[i]mplicit in the system's concern with parole violations is the notion that the parolee is entitled to retail his liberty as long as he substantially abides by the conditions of his parole."[3]

Pretrial diversion is not unlike probation and parole in that it is a program designed to put a person in the free community under certain restraints. In diversion, however, the state's interest in terminating a person's treatment is not as substantial as in probation or parole. In the latter cases the person stands convicted of a criminal offense; the danger of his freedom to the community has already been established. In diversion the person remains convicted of nothing although in some programs he may have entered a guilty plea.

Of course, diversion may justify certain conditions that would not be similar to those imposed on parolees or probationers. The nature of drug treatment may suggest the designation of a procedure for determining if the divertee is progressing satisfactorily, and it may require a recognition that such a determination may not achieve the same certainty that violation of many parole conditions allows. On the other hand, the divertee, unlike the parolee or probationer, waives certain constitutional rights prior to diversion. His interest in knowing in advance what activity will justify termination of his treatment program is substantial. Thus, while the nature of the conditions may differ from those of parole or probation, the requirement that they be stipulated in advance remains an important aspect in evaluating the fairness of a diversion program.

Failure of Treatment as Grounds for Termination

At some point the state has an interest in terminating a diversion-treatment program when a divertee does not respond to treatment for his addiction. The problem of defining with the required degree of particularity when this "failure" exists may create real legal problems for program planners. If the definition of failure is too vague, the entire revocation proceeding will be open to challenge for arbitrariness.

The giving of notice and the conduct of a hearing on termination will be simplified if medical "failure" as a cause for termination has been defined by an objective standard; such a definition might, for example, be stated in terms of a maximum acceptable number of heroin-positive urine tests during each week or month of the diversionary period. Such specificity may not be constitutionally required; a general finding of "unsuitability for treatment" may be a constitutionally sufficient cause for the termination of diversion.[4] But the adoption of objective standards of medical failure will allow unambiguous advance notification to prospective divertees of the conduct which is expected of them. Controversies at termination hearings over the propriety of subjective standards thus will be minimized.

In practice, of course, the use of fixed standards for medical failure may prove unfeasible since treatment personnel generally are accustomed to gauge their patient's progress subjectively and individually. But if the assessment of medical success or failure in each divertee's case is left to the discretion of treatment personnel, the divertee facing termination should be notified not only of their negative subjective assessment but also of the hard "evidence" on which it is based. He should have the opportunity to challenge not only the validity of the evidence but also the propriety of the conclusion drawn from it and the process by which they were drawn. Given the professional controversy that characterizes the field of drug-abuse treatment, there exists a real possibility that diversion-termination hearings may degenerate into contests over therapeutic theory and terminology.[5]

Even where an objective standard of medical failure is employed, the proceedings at a termination hearing can be expected to touch upon areas of expert medical dispute. Termination hearings can be expected to involve addict–divertees' claims that they have been inappropriately referred or inadequately treated, and these claims will not always be obviously frivolous. The officer presiding over the termination hearing should exercise his power to re-refer failing divertees to other more intensive or more restrictive therapeutic programs.[6] Although the divertee's constitutional right to re-referral may be merely speculative, the practical wisdom of dealing with "good faith" treatment failures through means short of final termination appears clear and may avoid some difficult legal problems.

Procedures for Termination

A defendant who voluntarily participates in a diversion program has a substantial interest in retaining his diverted status through to final successful completion of the treatment program. Attendant on a loss of such status are relative disadvantages in a subsequent prosecution and the possibility of a negative presentence report if the divertee is subsequently convicted, leading to incarceration. The prospect of termination thus threatens a "grievous loss" for which procedural fairness becomes essential.[7] The difficult question is the extent of the procedural protections available in a diversion termination context. It would appear that one of two lines of cases would be analogous. In *Morrissey* v. *Brewer*,[8] *Gagnon* v. *Scarpelli*,[9] and *Mempha* v. *Rhay*,[10] the Supreme Court articulated the process due in parole and probation revocation procedures. In *Wolff* v. *McDonnell*[11] the Court determined on a different and less demanding standard for prison disciplinary hearings revoking good-time credits.

The procedural standards for parole and probation revocation set forth by the Court in *Morrissey* and *Gagnon* might well be the minimum standards by which diversion-termination actions are gauged. These decisions recognize a legitimate state interest in economy and efficiency during the proceedings. However, this interest must be balanced against the demands of essential fairness, which require a procedure directed to insure that facts upon which a possible termination is based are accurate and reliable. In the parole and probation revocation proceedings, the court required a preliminary "reasonable cause" hearing by a neutral referee before an individual's privileged status is even temporarily curtailed, as by arrest and detention. Then if revocation is determined to be appropriate, a full revocation hearing is in order before the individual's status is finally terminated.

If the termination of participation in a pretrial-intervention program would generally not curtail the participant's liberty, as by arrest or detention, it is doubtful whether a preliminary "reasonable cause" hearing is essential. Rather, the due process requisite could be satisfied in one proceeding. The elements of this hearing should include, as outlined in *Morrissey:*

(a) written notice of the claimed violations . . .; (b) disclosure . . . of evidence against him; (c) opportunity to be heard in person and to present witnesses and documentary evidence; (d) the right to confront and cross-examine witnesses (unless the hearing officer specifically finds good cause for not allowing confrontation); (e) a "neutral and detached" hearing body . . .; and (f) a written statement by the fact-finders as to the evidence relied on and reasons for revocation.[12]

Where the court makes the decision to divert, it is the logical instrument to pass on issues of termination. In other cases, the revocation function would presumably be exercised by the prosecutor's office or program personnel. A "neutral" hearing officer is required. The program staff members who have gathered the facts upon which the decision to bring the termination proceeding is made, and have made the decision to apply for termination, would not meet the required impartiality standard. The court has recognized that prior involvement in some aspect of a case will not necessarily bar a welfare official from acting as a decision maker, but that official should not, however, have participated in making the determination under review.[13] If the same guarantee could be made in a hearing conducted by the prosecutor's office or staff personnel, then it would arguably meet existing due process standards.

As to the constitutional necessity of assistance of counsel in revocation proceedings, the Court in *Gagnon* concluded there was no absolute right to counsel but that it should be furnished on a case-by-case inquiry of necessity. Thus, analogizing probation revocation to revocation of diversionary status, counsel should be provided when, after a request is made, the defendant enters:

. . . a timely and colorable claim (i) that he has not committed the alleged violation of the conditions upon which he is at liberty or (ii) that even if the violation is a matter of public record or is uncontested, there are substantial reasons which justified or mitigated the violation . . . and that the reasons are complex or otherwise difficult to develop or present . . . (T)he responsible agency also should consider, especially in doubtful cases, whether the probationer appears to be capable of speaking effectively for himself.[14]

There may, however, be a basis for a *right* to counsel, for a termination hearing occurs at a "stage of a criminal proceeding where substantial rights of a criminal accused may be affected", the traditional test for the constitutional right to counsel.[15] Apart from the substantial interest the participant has in preserving his status, as well as the real and potential disabilities attaching upon termination of that status, other disabilities may arise that point to the need for, if not the right to, effective assistance of counsel. For example, statements made by the participant, as where the basis for the hearing is a rearrest or continued use of drugs, could be used in a subsequent prosecution unless a statutory privilege exists. The burden on the state in providing the opportunity for counsel would not be great, either (i) because the divertee may already have counsel, or (ii) because the right to counsel would in any event attach shortly thereafter if the defendant were to be prosecuted.

In *Wolff* v. *McDonnell*,[16] the Supreme Court applied a modified form of procedural regularity to prison disciplinary hearings where good time credits are revoked. The Court held that in such proceedings the inmate's right to present evidence in his defense is subject to the right of the administration to deny him that right if it will jeopardize institutional safety or correctional goals. The Court rejected the inmate's claim to the right to confront and cross-examine witnesses, and while indicating that counsel–substitute may be appropriate in some complex cases, stated that representation by an attorney was not required. The Court specifically refused to adopt the full range of *Morrissey* standards, primarily because of the prison environment that the Court categorized as one of tension, frustration, resentment, and despair, in which the relationships among inmates, and between inmates and staff, would not allow for a full adversary procedure.

Diversion bears little resemblance to the prison disciplinary procedures although it is, in all relevant respects, substantially similar to parole and probation. The defendant is released to the community on conditions and can be terminated upon violation of those conditions. He is at liberty, unlike the prison inmate who is confined. The tensions and frustrations existent in the prison are not found in the diversion situation. Furthermore, the divertee has waived several constitutional rights to obtain his status and should deserve at least the same procedural formalities as a parolee who has already been convicted of a criminal offense.

Results of Termination

A final issue relating to the termination of addict diversion is raised by the practice of treating a divertee's failure to live up to program standards as a per se disqualification from further program participation. As a matter of law, therapeutic policy, or both, re-referral rather than final termination of diversionary status may be the more appropriate outcome of an inquiry into the circumstances of a divertee's failure. As previously noted, there are equal protection arguments against mechanical exclusionary criteria that limit eligibility for diversion in the first instance on the basis of prior criminal records. These arguments apply with perhaps greater force to program designs or policies that make diversionary status automatically terminable upon mere rearrest without conviction.

Particular arrests during the diversionary period may amount to good cause for termination. Where, for example, rearrest is followed by detention, or where the new charge involves serious alleged drug-trafficking violations, a rational relationship might be found between disqualification for diversion and the circumstances of the new arrest. As a general matter, however, no administrative or therapeutic justification appears for regarding all rearrested addict–divertees as a disfavored class — especially when they assert their innocence on the new charges. There are strong policy considerations favoring the practice of rediverting many of these rearrested addict divertees, at least where there is a showing that they have made substantial progress toward rehabilitation. Drug-related criminality — like drug dependence itself — is a chronic condition as well as an acute one. It would be unrealistic, and perhaps counterproductive, to expect all addict–divertees to achieve a complete alteration of behavior immediately after being referred to treatment.

Unsuccessful performance in a diversion project should not automatically warrant the defendant's pretrial detention, even if the defendant is returned to the criminal process.[17] His failure in the program may or may not reflect on whether he will attend his future court appearances. Instead, the committing officer should determine first that the conditions set initially or other less restrictive conditions cannot reasonably insure the future appearance of the defendant (and, where "dangerousness" is a legitimate concern in pretrial-release decision-making, the safety of the community). It may seem tenuous to say that violations of diversion-project standards generally indicate greater risks before trial, warranting more restrictive conditions; such violations, however, can reflect adversely upon an individual defendant. Since discretion in setting conditions of release is with the court and is rarely disturbed on appeal, the former divertee's chances of avoiding jail detention rest primarily with the committing officer and his review of whether less restrictive conditions will suffice after diversion participation has been terminated.

Notes

1. Santobello v. New York, 404 U.S. 257 (1971). In some programs the divertee does not deal with a member of the prosecutor's immediate staff but with the staff of a diversion program. However, the basis for dis-

cussion regarding the possibility of diversion is promised acts by the prosecutor, that is, dismissing or suspending prosecution. Thus, the plea bargaining cases should be applicable regardless of whether there is direct prosecutor involvement in the negotiations.

2. In the guilty plea situation the court accepting the plea would have to be satisfied that the defendant knew the consequences of his plea. North Carolina v. Alford, 400 U.S. 25 (1970). See also FED. R. CRIM. P. 11.

3. 408 U.S. 471, 479 (1972).

4. For a discussion of the analogous—and unresolved—issue of lack of specificity and unconstitutional vagueness in parole conditions *see* Comment, *The Parole System,* 120 U. PA. L. REV. 282, 310–11 (1971).

5. An additional problem is created if the treatment program is governed by section 408 of the Federal Drug Abuse Office and Treatment Act of 1972, 21 U.S.C. § 1175. That provision and the regulations thereunder prohibit treatment staff to provide records of his progress unless the patient consents. Thus, diversion programs must provide a mechanism for obtaining written consent of divertees if they seek to have treatment success be a condition for continued participation. *See* 21 C.F.R. § 1401.24 (1974).

6. In programs where the divertee is initially referred to a multiple-modality program, of course, re-referral at the termination hearing may be unnecessary or impossible; before reporting a medical failure, a program employing a number of distinct therapeutic techniques may itself afford the divertee an opportunity to find the one best suited to him through testing, counselling, and trial and error.

7. Goldberg v. Kelley, 397 U.S. 254 (1970).

8. 408 U.S. 471 (1972).

9. 411 U.S. 778 (1973).

10. 389 U.S. 128 (1967).

11. 418 U.S. 539 (1974).

12. Morrissey v. Brewer, *supra* note 8, at 489.

13. Goldberg v. Kelley, *supra* note 7.

14. Gagnon v. Scarpelli, *supra* note 9, at 790.

15. See Chapter 4, *supra.*

16. *Supra* note 11.

17. See page 58, *supra* for a discussion of treatment as a condition of pretrial release.

8 Conclusion

The foregoing analysis suggests that in a variety of ways addict-diversion programs as presently operated raise serious legal issues involving the rights of those they are designed to serve. It could, of course, be argued that the seriousness of the points raised is tempered by the fact that the alternative to diversion is very often detention, prosecution, and ultimate confinement in prison. But the choice is not that narrow, and the alternative to programs that invade constitutionally protected liberties may be similar programs that are altered to avoid such invasions. It may be true that the latter promises fewer successes, that they will not serve as high a percentage of those arrested, that they will require costlier procedures. However, it is also true that society has higher values than the treatment of drug addiction.

It is instructive to recall that the maximum-security prison was hailed as a humanitarian alternative to physical punishment. The seeming beneficence of pretrial diversion ought not serve as a justification for diminishing civil rights. It ought, rather, to alert us to the possibility that in our rush to reap the benefits we may ignore the implications of our actions.

There is nothing in the analysis here that suggests pretrial addict-diversion programs are inherently suspect or are incapable of being constitutionally designed. It must also be recognized that there are no existing cases that directly call into question procedures now employed in most programs. In many areas of constitutional law, diversion techniques fall uncomfortably between diverging lines of authority. The analysis here attempts to set out the various legal perspectives from which these techniques can be evaluated and to offer the major arguments suggesting caution.

About the Authors

Harvey S. Perlman is a professor of law at the University of Virginia. He received the B.A. and the J.D. from the University of Nebraska. He has served as acting director of the Nebraska Commission on Law Enforcement and Criminal Justice and as a staff associate for the Task Force on Corrections of the National Advisory Commission on Criminal Justice Standards and Goals. He is a reporter to both the American Bar Association Joint Committee on the Legal Status of Prisoners and the Special Committee on the Uniform Corrections Code of the National Conference of Commissioners on Uniform State Laws.

Peter A. Jaszi is a member of the staff of the Institute for Advanced Studies in Justice, American University Law School. He received the B.A. and the J.D. from Harvard University. He is the research director for the Task Force on Disorders and Terrorism for the National Advisory Commission on Criminal Justice Standards and Goals.